MW01298363

Choosing to Live

Enduring the Loss of a Loved One

Jerry D. Campbell

ARCHWAY
PUBLISHING

Copyright © 2014 Jerry D. Campbell.

All rights reserved. No part of this book may be used or reproduced by any means, graphic, electronic, or mechanical, including photocopying, recording, taping or by any information storage retrieval system without the written permission of the publisher except in the case of brief quotations embodied in critical articles and reviews.

Archway Publishing books may be ordered through booksellers or by contacting:

Archway Publishing
1663 Liberty Drive
Bloomington, IN 47403
www.archwaypublishing.com
1-(888)-242-5904

Because of the dynamic nature of the Internet, any web addresses or links contained in this book may have changed since publication and may no longer be valid. The views expressed in this work are solely those of the author and do not necessarily reflect the views of the publisher, and the publisher hereby disclaims any responsibility for them.

Any people depicted in stock imagery provided by Thinkstock are models, and such images are being used for illustrative purposes only. Certain stock imagery © Thinkstock.

ISBN: 978-1-4808-1013-6 (sc)
ISBN: 978-1-4808-1015-0 (hc)
ISBN: 978-1-4808-1014-3 (e)

Library of Congress Control Number: 2014914530

Printed in the United States of America.

Archway Publishing rev. date: 08/15/2014

CONTENTS

PREFACE

In going about our daily activities, we plan for life, not for death. It's not that we are unaware that death can happen at any moment, but because we simply do not dwell on it. Until something happens that forces us to think otherwise, we take for granted that we will wake up in the morning and that those we love will do the same. When death comes to someone we love, therefore, we are often catapulted into deep, disconsolate grief.

This book is intended to help readers who have lost someone very close. It is based on my own experience after the unexpected death of my wife, Veta, in April of 2010. I began writing it after a friend suggested that telling others how I dealt with the process of grieving might be helpful to them. I could not know whether a process that worked for me would be useful to anyone else, but I decided to give the idea the benefit of a doubt.

In the book, I offer the viewpoint that knowing something about what to expect during grief and setting certain expectations immediately after loss occurs can help you get through grief with a healthier outcome. Faced with the shocking reality of Veta's death, I immediately felt an urgency to find a method for guiding myself through the grief process in a way that would allow me both to grieve and to continue to function professionally. Since I did not know of such a method, I developed the simple approach described here. Though it may be far from perfect, I found that having a way to understand and manage grief was of immense help as I dealt with the loss of my wife, Veta.

The method described here made sense for me because of both my health history and my work history. My health history has required that I always be self-aware, and my work history has always put me at the mercy of a full and demanding calendar for the ordering of my days, weeks, and years. I am accustomed to being guided by a schedule. Thus, I created the grief calendar described in what follows, and it helped me make it through the traumatic experience. I have written this with the hope that it will be of help to you.

The book, therefore, is partly my suggestions about steps to deal with grief and partly about the description of my own grief experience. Because this mixes how-to suggestions with the story of my own grief, I have arranged it in a particular way. It would be most helpful, of course, for someone to read this well in advance of the loss of a loved one. In reality, however, I know that if it is consulted, it will most likely be after such a loss happens. So I have placed a summary of my suggestions early in the book for quick reference. Following that I have told my own story. Finally, I conclude with some observations of what I learned as a result of dealing with grief and subsequently writing about it.

Since this relates the story of *my* grief, it is fashioned around the circumstances of my life and work as they occurred during the period described. I want to emphasize, however, that such circumstances are different for each and every person and that the grief process will take place regardless of what your situation may be. Because I traveled extensively during my grief, largely as part of my work, I hope that the fact of my traveling will not be a distraction. A needed uplift from the natural world, for instance, can be experienced walking on a tree-lined street, in a park, or sitting in a secluded patio—anywhere you can see grass or trees, hear birds, or feel the wind. If you have children and are in need of some time alone, seek the help of a friend, neighbor, or family member. No matter what your circumstances may be, taking a deliberate approach to grieving can, I believe, help you get through it, and it can be done within the context of your own personal situation.

I am profoundly sorry if you are reading this because you have lost someone close. If such is the case, you are beginning one of the most challenging but common emotional experiences that humans undergo. Nonetheless, if you make up your mind now to deal with grief in a healthy and self-conscious manner, I am confident that you can find your way to a new and fulfilling next phase in your life.

Chapter 1: What to Do When Loss Occurs

When someone very close to you dies, you are faced with one of the greatest emotional challenges that we humans can know: dealing with death. It is not a challenge you were seeking, but one that is thrust upon you. Even if you have been expecting your loved one's death, it requires an emotional adjustment.

Simply put, the challenge is getting through sometimes overwhelming grief in order to return to a healthy, fulfilling life. Though this challenge may be described as largely emotional in character, it can be severe enough to have serious implications for your physical well-being. For this reason, it is important for you to understand grieving and to exercise a degree of self-control as you grieve.

Though there probably will be unique aspects to the way *you* respond to the death of someone close, it is likely that you will also experience a number of emotional responses that humans share. Because emotional responses common to the human experience of loss have been described by others, it is possible for you to know in advance what you will most likely experience as you grieve. And knowing even in general terms what to expect provides you with the opportunity to be more deliberate and self-aware as you grieve. It also makes it more likely that you will meet the challenge of grieving and return to a healthy, fulfilling life.

When a Loved One Dies

Make the decision to live!

When someone close to you dies, make the decision that you will go on living.

Do this especially if the person you lost was your spouse, significant other, or a close family member. Suddenly confronted with the reality of being without the one you have lost, there is real danger that you may feel like your own life is no longer worth living. You may feel like just giving up and dying. It is urgent, therefore, that you focus on these feelings and make the decision to live within the first few days after your loved one dies.

Because this critical decision falls on you at precisely the time you are in shock, when you are feeling numb, find someone to talk with about this. Seek out a clergyperson, a counselor, a family member, a friend—someone who can help you focus on the positive value of going on with your life.

I cannot overemphasize the importance of consciously making the decision that you will go on living and setting yourself the goal of getting through your grief.

Get a sense, an understanding, of what you will be feeling.

Take time shortly after the loss of your loved one to learn how others have described the process of grief.

If possible, buy or borrow a copy of the book *On Grief and Grieving: Finding the Meaning of Grief Through the Five Stages of Loss* (New York, Scribner, 2005), co-authored by Elizabeth

Kübler-Ross and David Kessler (hereafter referred to simply as *Grief*).

Read the first chapter. It is only eighteen pages long, and you can easily read it in a short while. Learn about the five stages of loss so that you can understand better what you are already beginning to feel and why.

If possible, buy the book so that you can write on it and reread the descriptions of the stages as often as you need to.

Create your personal calendar for dealing with the stages of loss.

In spite of the fact that *Grief* helped me identify the stages I would be facing, I felt a clear, even desperate need for a tool or structure that would allow me to compartmentalize my personal life from my professional life to some degree so that I could give adequate attention to both. So I decided to build the five-stage grieving process into my schedule for the rest of the year. By doing so, I could insure that I fulfilled my professional responsibilities while also scheduling adequate time for each stage of the *grief work*. I found this technique extremely helpful, so I go into greater detail about how I did it in chapter 4. Here's a brief summary:

Make a schedule for the next several months for how you will deal with each of the five stages of loss.

Put your schedule for progressing through the five stages on your calendar. If you are working, put it on your work calendar. My choice of eight months (through the end of the calendar year) was adequate, but it was also arbitrary. The point is to allow yourself as much time as needed to deal with a very difficult and emotionally exhausting process. The stages and my own brief description of them are:

- *Denial*: Feeling as if it just can't be true; experiencing utter disbelief;
- *Anger*: Being mad at yourself and any other individuals or agencies related to the death of your loved one;
- *Bargaining*: Trying to make a deal with God or fate to make it not so;
- *Depression*: Slipping into a malaise characterized by loss of energy and focus;
- *Acceptance*: Coming to terms with the reality of loss in a way that allows you to move on.

Schedule time to focus attention on each stage described in *Grief*. Make sure that you have plenty of time scheduled outside of work to think about or to talk with a friend about each of the stages. Don't avoid or skip dealing carefully and thoughtfully with any stage, even if it means reexamining your most fundamental beliefs, whether they derive from a religious tradition or from a secular viewpoint. In fact, rather than fearing a reexamination of your assumptions about what you believe, welcome it as a part of your inner work, because delving into those assumptions can lead to a deeper, more mature faith or belief system.

Remember that the five stages represent an effort to identify in general the feelings that follow the loss of a loved one, and that they may not precisely match your own unique response. Don't hesitate to modify your description of the stages to be in line with what you are feeling. Also remember that the calendar is yours to change, lengthen, or shorten to match your own grief work.

At the end of these five stages outlined in *Grief*, I found there to be a sixth stage that I call *Growth*. This growth is the result of spending time reflecting, perhaps writing about your own grief process. It is a result of dealing intimately and thoughtfully with your own emotions and the issues that the death of a loved one involves. It is helpful at the very outset to be aware that you may experience personal growth as the result of your pain if you set your intention to do so.

As you develop your own grief calendar, think of your grief work as a new job, and actively work on it.

Set aside regular times to think and reflect
on your grief, and begin today.

Don't underestimate the challenge you are facing, but don't fear it.

Be aware that you are entering a process from which you will emerge with a life that cannot and will not be the same as it was before. Take on the challenge of deep grief, therefore, with heightened self-awareness and self-reflection. Be aware that in time you can again find joy in living, but it requires that you find a way to be at peace with your loss. Only after I had been in grief for some time did I manage to write a short meditation that helped me immensely. (*Grief,* 94–95.) Don't be afraid to write out your guilt, your anger, and your struggles and to find positive ways to face them. In doing so, you will begin to heal from your loss.

If the death of your loved one leaves you alone, you will have the additional task of getting comfortable being by yourself. It may help to think of being alone as a gift of solitude rather than forced loneliness. Work at getting comfortable with solitude.

Set aside time regularly to stop and evaluate your progress throughout the process. In my case, since I was suddenly living alone, I set aside two times each workday to focus on where I was in my grief process. One of these times was the first thirty minutes after I awoke in the morning. I kept *Grief* on the bedside table and would review the short description of the stage I was working through. I would ask myself if my feelings fit the description or if they were different, and I tried to understand what "progressing through the stage" would mean for me. At the end of the morning time, I would turn to my work calendar and attempt to focus on my work agenda.

The second time I set aside to reflect on workdays was the first hour after I arrived home from work. I had deliberately compartmentalized grief so that it did not disrupt my work, so I needed to take time to reengage with my grieving. I would usually start by asking myself if any of my feelings stood out or if anything in particular was bothering me and go from there. This became a good time for me to review previous stages and was so helpful that I suggest that you make such review a frequent practice.

In addition, if you are able, set aside blocks of time to reinforce your grief work through reading or talking with friends or family members. (I used Saturday mornings.) This is especially helpful if you feel like you are stuck or can't resolve certain feelings. Having time available and using it to seek assistance will help you think more clearly and honestly about how you are doing and help you make emotional progress. Don't hurry; give yourself all the time necessary—a year or more—to identify what will be your new normal.

Strongly consider having a memorial service, funeral, or
other formal means of celebrating your loved one's life.

Arrange for some kind of formal service (a memorial service, funeral service, wake, or the like) in which family and friends can join you in celebrating the life and mourning the passing of your loved one. Even if you have not cared for the various formal means of marking someone's death, I think you will find it helpful and well worth doing. If you don't wish to plan such a service yourself, you can readily enlist the help of friends, family, or professionals. Not only will such a service prove beneficial to you, it will also help all others who may wish to observe the death of your loved one in a concrete and meaningful way. I can't say precisely why such services are beneficial, but I can testify to the significantly positive impact of Veta's memorial services on family, friends, and me.

Don't drown out your grief with TV, music, web surfing, or other forms of distraction.

Avoid using the TV or other forms of distraction to prevent yourself from dealing with uncomfortable feelings of grief.

You cannot think or reflect on your grief work when you are distracted by any of a great variety of contemporary forms of activity that occupy your attention. Of course, engaging in entertainment is okay—just not to the degree that it interferes with your grief work.

When you enter your regularly scheduled time to think or pray about your own feelings and the stages of loss, turn off the distractions.

Don't turn to alcohol or drugs as a solace for emotional pain.

Be aware from the moment of your loss that your susceptibility to abuse of alcohol and drugs (including prescription drugs) is heightened—especially if you are alone.

Even though alcohol and drugs may seem to blunt your emotional pain, when you are under the influence of either you are less capable of dealing honestly with your feelings and making progress through the stages of loss. If possible, therefore, be careful not to develop a dependence on drugs, and limit drinking of alcohol to times when you are with others, and then exercise moderation. If you are unavoidably alone, put clear limits on your use of drugs and alcohol and adhere to your limits.

If you have any doubts about being able to adhere to your limits, talk with your doctor, psychologist, or other similarly qualified individual immediately. No matter how much it may seem to help, turning to the short term comfort provided by drugs or alcohol will in the long run endanger and possibly ruin your health and happiness.

Don't hesitate to get help.

It is not a sign of weakness to turn to others for support.

Let family and friends provide assistance and support in any ways that they can. Doing so will not only help you, but will also help them in dealing with their own grief.

If you follow a religious tradition, seek out one of its leaders. Religious organizations have accumulated wisdom about and ways of understanding and dealing with death. Make an effort to talk with a knowledgeable person to whom you look up as a spiritual leader. And you need not be an adherent to a religious tradition to seek the help of most religious leaders.

If you have no association with organized religion and prefer to seek help elsewhere, turn to someone you trust and respect, perhaps a health care provider or licensed counselor, for advice and support. Of course, you can also take this approach if you are a member of a religious organization.

Take care of the practical tasks.

When your loved one dies, even though you may be dazed, there are several important practical tasks to be carried out.

You don't have to figure these out on your own; you can find practical advice about what to do by searching on the Internet. Using Google or some other search engine, search for: [things to do after someone dies]. One such site you will find is offered by the US Department of Health and Human Services: http://www.nia.nih.gov/health/publication/end-life-helping-comfort-and-care/things-do-after-someone-dies. You can easily find a number of such sites.

These do-list items are very helpful, and some of the tasks identified are critically important. Use the suggestions to make your own list. Let family and friends help with the practical matters when possible. But remember that taking care of some routine matters can remind that you are still engaged in life, and that can be reassuring during your distress over your loss.

LaVeta Dea Sinclair Campbell

Chapter 2: Introducing Veta

Chances are …
When they want to see
How true love should be
They'll just look at us*

An Obituary (Read at Veta's Memorial Service)

LaVeta Dea Sinclair was born in Plainview, Texas, on January 28, 1946. It was a windy day. Of course, every day in Plainview is a windy day. She made many lifelong friends in Plainview before that wind embedded itself in Veta's character. Blowing like the Spirit, Veta moved to Abilene, Texas. She married Jerry Campbell on December 22, 1967, and graduated from the Methodist-affiliated McMurry College in 1968. She made many lifelong friends.

The wind came again. From 1968 to 1971 Veta found herself in Durham, North Carolina, where she taught elementary school in order to put Jerry through graduate programs at both Duke University and the University of North Carolina at Chapel Hill. She made many lifelong friends in North Carolina.

The next gust landed her in Denver, Colorado, where she

---

* "Look at Us"; Larry Bastian, Buddy Cannon, Morgan, and Vince Gill; recorded by Vince Gill in 1991.

worked at the United Methodist headquarters of the Rocky Mountain Conference of the United Methodist Church. There she was not only a supportive wife, but she became a mother in 1973, when Denise joined the family. In Denver, she made a wonderful home and many lifelong friends.

But the wind came again, and Veta, Jerry, and Denise moved to Dallas in 1980. There she taught first and third grades at Highland Park Elementary School, earned a masters degree from East Texas State University, served as a dedicated mother, and was the perfect professional's wife. She also managed the family's social life and made many lifelong friends.

The Spirit-wind was also strong in Dallas, and it blew through her life again, taking the family back to North Carolina. There she again taught school but eventually became the manager of the Purple Puddle, a gift store owned by a friend. She continued as the supportive wife of a senior university administrator, a loving mother, and the manager of the family's social life. And there she became the "church lady," serving many important lay roles within the University United Methodist Church in Chapel Hill, North Carolina. And—you may have guessed it by now—she made many lifelong friends.

Never say that you would never move to crazy, crowded Southern California. That Spirit-wind is unpredictable! And so Veta found herself, with Jerry, moving to Pasadena, where she functioned as the perfect hostess-wife of a USC dean. She also became an essential presence and leader within the First United Methodist Church, Pasadena—the church lady at her best. She missed Denise, who was finishing college in North Carolina and was thrilled when Denise chose to come to Southern California after College. Who, after all, could stay across the continent from so fetching a mom as Veta? In Pasadena, Veta, of course, made many lifelong friends. But she also began to create networks of her friends—introducing them to one another, making friends of friends.

Finally that Spirit-wind blew Veta out to Upland to become the first lady of Claremont School of Theology. There, as the perfect president's wife, she continued to build her legacy of friend-making. Most of you here today are part of her network of friends. She finally turned this friend-making back to the restless, always moving Spirit on April 19, 2010. Now it is up to all of us to continue her legacy.

Veta

We met the summer before our senior year in high school. We were both working at Plains Drug Store in downtown Plainview, Texas. Veta was a cashier at the main cash register, and I was the stock boy. There was a store policy against employee dating, and we became the first couple to violate the policy. We were sufficiently attracted to one another that we talked it over and decided a date was worth the risk. We didn't want to do it on the sly, however, so we simply told the owner that we were going out on a date. And we did.

Since I was a farm boy and she a city girl, I took her on a dangerous, nighttime "watermelon stealing" date. She was quite nervous and didn't know where we were in the dark expanse of Northwest Texas farm country, but even though I told her tales of irate farmers exchanging lead for rock salt in shotgun shells in order to keep watermelon thieves away, she was up for the adventure. Just to be on the safe side, of course, I took her to the farm of our nearest neighbor. The dangerous plan dissolved, however, when we encountered the neighbor's land manager, who even in the dark greeted me by name and told me where the best melons could be found. With some relief, she called me a fake but said she could tolerate it because we had gotten two really nice watermelons. Just for fun, we carved our initials on one of them and left it on the steps of the house where the owner of Plains Drug Store lived. At work the next week, Veta explained to him and his wife what we had done, and afterwards, he did away with the no employee dating policy.

Veta was remarkably self-sufficient. Her father had four children by his first wife who had died from blood poisoning and left him to raise the children. He had subsequently married Veta's mom, and Veta was their only child together. In some of the difficult drought years before she was born, her dad had lost his farm and resorted to working for the county maintaining unpaved roads. Shortly before her death, Veta penned the following poem about her father and her.

On a doorstep
There I am on my dad's knee
on the doorstep of the old white frame house.
1207 Portland.
Phone was 1565J. Sometimes neighbors used it for calls.
Not everyone had phones then. Short calls. Had a party
    line.
That could be fun.

Five kids, two, sometimes three, adults crammed in.
Cow in the back, some chickens, too.
Fresh milk. Chicken's neck wrung for Sunday.
Never could stand that.
And lots of cats and a dog.
Bedlam.

It looks peaceful in the photo.
He's old for having a little girl.
Former life still chasing him in the lines of his face.
The losses etched deep.
Farm dusted out;
First wife, son dead. Too young to go.
How can you perish from blood poisoning—a cut with old
    kitchen knife?
Can't a young boy be saved from death of appendicitis?

He had a weight about his small frame—
Open collared, smoking a cigarette, kind of handsome.
Maybe a little relaxed.
I think he loved that little girl with big eyes and ringlets.
Seems like for that moment he was a little hopeful.
Some of the waves of past misery washed past for now.
Signs of some newness, begin again.

At 1207 Portland

Veta's mom worked as well, as bookkeeper for a farm equipment dealer, and though they never had extra financial resources, they got by.

Veta was considerably younger than her four half-siblings, so in certain ways her early years shared elements of being an only child. One example that she talked about often was her need to walk more than a mile each way to and from school beginning in the first grade. Plainview is situated at the base of the Texas Panhandle, which meant that she walked through bitterly cold weather in the winter. But what she remembered most vividly was not the cold but the constantly blowing sand

and dust that, whether cold or hot, stung her legs and bothered her eyes. The wind never rested, and it became something of a nemesis for her. She was always conscious of the wind, and perhaps her early experience walking in the wind was the reason she preferred to wear pants when it was appropriate. She also remembered feeling vulnerable as she walked. Never, however, did she waver. She loved school and was determined to go. I believe that early experience accounted for some of the self-sufficiency and determination she exhibited throughout the rest of her life.

Though I called Veta a city girl, Plainview was a small town of less than 20,000 people, situated in the midst of cotton farms. It didn't take long to drive from one end of the town to the other. In those days, Plainview had one indoor movie theater and one outdoor drive-in movie. There was a drive-in hamburger place that constituted a turn-around point on the endless cycle that we and other high school age young people would drive on Saturday nights as we car-dated back and forth on Fifth Street.

I think it was the small town and endless cycle on the same street that gave Veta a desire to travel. No one I have known loved new places more than she did. Whether it was Zion National Park in Utah, Trevi Fountain in Rome, or the Great Wall of China, she anticipated each trip we took, read about the destination, and thoroughly enjoyed the experience. She preferred savoring the experience to taking photos, and she could recall an amazing amount of detail about the places we visited. She was the best personal tour guide one could ever hope to have.

That small town may also have sparked her intense interest in people and given her the remarkable ability to remember their names, including the names and number of their children.

She could also remember what people were wearing the first time she met them, what they wore on special occasions, and when to send their birthday cards. This talent made her an indispensable presence in my roles as library director, dean, and president.

Sometime after Veta's death, a longtime friend asked me what I would say were her major contributions. It was an open-ended question without qualifying contributions to what, and it was a wonderful question. The answer to that question may be the best way to provide a glimpse into just who Veta was and why so many people loved her.

For me, Veta's greatest contribution was raising our daughter Denise. I was fully engaged in my work, and Veta was the parent on duty most of the time. In her parental role, she was exceptionally attentive and caring, and being an elementary school teacher herself, knew how to challenge, motivate, and reward Denise. She was also a better disciplinarian than me, and she was intent on raising Denise in a way that gave her self-confidence, self-control, and independence. I am happy to say that Denise grew into a wonderful woman who makes a substantial contribution to society and who reflects all of the positive attributes that Veta had hoped she would.

In February 2004 I was in the Cleveland Clinic on the eve before having a complicated heart surgery, and I was asked what I would say was my greatest accomplishment. I responded without hesitation that it was Denise. Every one of the friends and family present knew that I was really testifying to the parenting work done by Veta. For me, helping Denise become the substantial person she is today stands as Veta's greatest contribution to our family and our culture.

But raising Denise was only the tip of a substantial iceberg of accomplishment. Indeed, Veta was intensely active socially.

Always interested in people, she was exceptionally good at remembering names, birthdays, and other personal details. She used her intimate knowledge of individuals to introduce strangers to one another who would soon become friends. In this way, she started book groups and dinner groups, and because we had lived in many different places, provided people who had moved with the names of contacts in their new locations. In addition to parenting, bringing people together and creating new sets of friends was another of Veta's great contributions to the communities in which she lived.

Similarly, she was a master at carrying out the public spousal roles that accompanied my positions as university librarian, dean, and most recently president of a graduate school, Claremont School of Theology. She attended public events, served as hostess at parties, and represented my office and the school at fundraising occasions and on school-sponsored trips. In recent years, she traveled with me to meetings where the spouses of presidents were included. She was gifted in such roles and always presented herself with dignity, poise, and confidence.

I was fortunate all those years that Veta was also terrific at homemaking. She took great pride in seeing that our home was a fresh, well-appointed, attractive, and comfortably welcoming place for both friends and strangers. She was a master magician in our home, or so I experienced and described it. She tended the "magic dresser" in which I found a never-ending supply of clean socks and fresh-smelling underclothes; she managed the "magic medicine cabinet" in which I always found fresh supplies of my prescriptions; and she operated a "magic kitchen" in which I continually encountered my favorite foods. She also took care of our finances, bills, and taxes.

So far, the above paragraphs only testify to the significant parenting, homemaking, spousal, and friend-making roles that Veta filled, but for almost twenty years of our married life she also taught elementary school. Her focus was first through third grades, and she was a masterful teacher. For each child, she could find the right balance between affection and discipline, and the result motivated each of her pupils to give their best effort in the classroom. She struggled over how to help "problem" children, and I don't remember that she ever had a pupil whose school performance she could not somehow improve. I am convinced that one of Veta's great contributions was to set many young people on a positive academic track as they began their public school experience. She, like other teachers of our children, is an unsung heroine for the role she played in mentoring tomorrow's leaders.

Her success at teaching, however, came at the cost of long and challenging hours of work both on and off the job. Veta insisted on spending the time necessary to be well-prepared in the classroom. For this reason, she reduced her teaching involvement after Denise was born in order to make certain that Denise would get adequate parental attention. She eventually gave up teaching when I took on a vice provost role at Duke University during Denise's high school years, but worked some hours with a friend who had opened what became a highly successful gift shop.

Veta had always loved church and had been regular in her attendance, but it was after she gave up teaching that she came to be referred to by her friends as the "church lady." Though her mom had been a Methodist, her dad was a Southern Baptist, and she was raised in the Southern Baptist tradition. She did not, however, find the theological strictures of Southern Baptist theology and church doctrine amenable to her own understanding and experience. Thus, when she became acquainted with the Methodist tradition after we married (I have been a lifelong Methodist), she observed that she had finally found a church that she could embrace. And that she did in every way.

So, at our home church in Chapel Hill, North Carolina, Veta became significantly involved as a layperson. She served on and chaired a variety of church committees, including the committee that was responsible for overseeing the church's staff. In addition, she served as lay leader of the congregation and became credentialed as a *Stephen Minister*, a layperson who essentially serves the role of a pastoral counselor for individuals in need.

After our move to Southern California, Veta continued her active church involvement in the Pasadena First United Methodist Church. While she played a number of important roles, perhaps the most significant and satisfying to her was chairing the committee overseeing the project for the renovation and earthquake retrofitting of that church's chapel. In the end, the effort she chaired improved the chapel by adding a second wall of windows, bringing it into compliance with contemporary building codes, and restoring the extraordinary beauty of the existing building. This was, perhaps the capstone of the kind of contribution that Veta made time and time again over the years in the communities in which we lived.

This brief introduction to Veta would not be complete without noting her deep love and affection for animals, particularly dogs. She adored dogs, and dogs loved her. Almost without exception, strange dogs would approach her and let her touch them. Rarely was there a dog, even a watchdog, that didn't sense and respond to her "dog charm." So naturally, beginning soon after we married, we had a succession of dogs in our family. Each was memorable and held a special place in Veta's heart. She would smile at the inclusion of this paragraph.

I am choosing to end this introduction to Veta with a few more of her poems so that you can know her through her own words.

Veta's Poems

Spring snow
'Midst the feathery flakes and brittle breezes
In imposing ivy towers,
Famed football field and gracious greenspace
Comes crashing hell on an April Monday.

Young minds scrambling and nimble bodies
Leaping to life, dodging death if they could.
Sacrificial old man, survivor of past horrors
Letting the young have their chance—as he once did.

Don't think there is no meaning here.
What resonates loudest is the Promise of Youth,
The Wisdom of Age. One day there will be plans again—
On some future Monday when the spring snow comes
    gently.

—April 17, 2006

Is it?

Is it possible
to see beyond,
to care outside
the boundaries of
our lives?

Is it something
to hope for and
to work toward
greater harmony in
our living?

Is it?

Is it in us
to lose ourselves,
to find another's viewpoint
in the age of
All about *me*?

Is it time
to face the needs,
to see the faces
and a better way
of living?

Is it?

—December 27, 2007

It's so simple now

It's so simple now to leave the house.

No tossing treats in just the right spot, no securing gates to block stairs,

No need to rush back home, no one eagerly awaiting my arrival.

It's so simple to leave the house

It's so simple to get to sleep at night.

No fur ball scratching at pillows, burrowing around, groaning as he does,

No need to share the space, no getting shoved into a mere slice of the bed.

It's so simple to get to sleep at night.

It's so simple, but it's so quiet, so still.

No barking at the pantry for a treat, no scooting the food dish 'round,

No snoring half the day, no blind eyes watching when awake.

It's too quiet, it's too still, it's too ordinary.

—August 15, 2009

Chapter 3: Encountering the Unthinkable

She ain't ashamed to be a woman, or afraid to be a friend.
I don't know the answer to the easy way
she opened every door in my mind.
But dreaming was as easy as believing it was never gonna end.
And loving her was easier than anything I'll ever do again.[*]

Unexpected Death

I was no stranger to the grief process, having experienced the death of my parents, other family members, and close friends, but never before had I been plunged so deeply into grief. It is not just an abstract idea in some expressions of commitment that "two shall become one;" it is a psychological reality that is manifested in enduring, successful relationships. In this case, Veta and I had been married for forty-two years and four months of the almost forty-seven years we were sweethearts. We had a wonderful, satisfying marriage in which we had learned to enjoy one another as lovers, partners, parents, and friends. Mutual agreement came easily to us with respect to almost every aspect of life, whether taste in food, family matters, travel, entertainment, or friends. So close had we become that even

[*] "Loving Her Was Easier"; Kris Kristofferson.

our worst disagreements had a way of ending well. Losing her was overwhelming.

Veta's death was entirely unexpected. Though we had known for several years that she had a somewhat mysterious disease called *sarcoidosis*, she was generally in good to excellent health. The cause of sarcoidosis is unknown, but in my words, it is a disease in which clumps of abnormal immune cells called *granulomas* form in many of the body's organs, including lymph nodes, lungs, liver, eyes, and skin. It most commonly affects the lungs, replacing healthy lung tissue with scar tissue granulomas, a condition referred to as *pulmonary fibrosis*.

Though Veta's sarcoidosis sometimes caused her to have a dry cough at night and several other mild symptoms, it was well under control. It did not noticeably limit her activity. She frequently traveled with me nationally and internationally and was busily active in our church and other local organizations. In other words, Veta was otherwise healthy, active, and vitally involved in home, church, and community. And she was fully supportive of my work and committed to her role as a president's wife. She made it possible for me to work incessantly without worrying about things at home. She exuded energy and efficiency.

Indeed, I was the one with a health issue and a shortened life expectancy.

I was born with a defective heart valve, an aortic valve that had two leaflets rather than the usual three. In my particular case, the leaflets became stiff and calcified by the time I had reached my teens so that they did not fully close. As a result, each time my heart pumped blood out to my body, the blood would regurgitate. This led to an enlarged heart, with symptoms sufficiently severe that I was not expected to live beyond my mid-teens. Unfortunately, that was at a time when heart surgery was in its infancy and prosthetic valves were not yet available.

Thus it was that at the age of thirteen (1958) I became the sixth experiment in repairing a congenitally deformed aortic valve by a team of pioneer heart surgeons, Dr. Michael DeBakey and Dr. Denton Cooley. It was to be the first of six open-heart surgeries over a period of forty-five years, with Veta at my side through five of them.

Talk of Ultimate Things

When I underwent my second heart surgery at the age of twenty-two, Veta was with me. For this reason, we talked about death deeply and often, but it was always the prospect of my death that prompted our conversations. Occasionally we would engage in an exchange in which I told Veta that my purpose in life was to make her happy, and her rejoinder was that her purpose in life was to keep me healthy. As things turned out, I like to think we both kept our parts of the bargain.

We prepared our first wills on the occasion of my third open-heart surgery (1978), when I was thirty-three and Veta was thirty-two. By that time, we had with us our daughter Denise. So we talked seriously about how Veta would go forward if I died. Veta learned everything there was to know about our finances and other important matters. Together we put our family affairs in order. This was a process that we repeated in 1987, 1990, and 2004.

In retrospect, I cannot overstate the importance of our periodic discussions of ultimate things. I don't know whether we would have had such conversations if my health circumstances had not required it. Even with a catalyst, conversations about death and related subjects are difficult. Death is not something we want to think about, especially when we are young. Talking about death is almost a cultural taboo. Such conversations evoke a primitive superstition that even mentioning death might awaken it and invite it in. It makes us want to knock on wood, hurry on, and talk of more pleasant subjects. I do know, however, that if we had not had those conversations about ultimate things, I would have been unprepared to make certain decisions as Veta's situation became critical. And I would never have found peace regarding whether my decisions matched her preferences.

Difficulties notwithstanding, therefore, there are reasons why we should seriously discuss death with those we love whatever our age—even when we are young. How else can we know our loved one's wishes with regard to certain important life and death issues? Each time it became necessary for me to undergo another heart surgery, I found myself urgently wanting Veta to know my thoughts and preferences about certain matters. Perhaps most importantly, I wanted her to know that I did not wish to be kept alive if it required being placed for the long term on a ventilator, and I wanted her to have the legal power to exercise what is often referred to as a *do not resuscitate* (DNR) order on my behalf.

I also wanted her to know that it would be my wish for her to remarry when I died. I didn't like to think of her as a long-grieving widow alone and sad. I wanted her to be happy and fulfilled. In addition, when our daughter was young, I wanted Veta to find someone who would fill the role of dad for Denise. So as I encountered each occasion requiring heart surgery, I felt a need to be certain Veta knew clearly how I felt.

In addition, so that she would not be at loose ends with regard to our family's personal matters, I wanted to be sure that Veta knew about where all our important papers were kept.

These included insurance policies, titles to cars and property, tax records, our personal finances, my retirement accounts, and so on. I wanted coping with my death not to be made more difficult because of lack of information about and complications with such matters.

As a result of our conversations about ultimate things, not only did Veta know my preferences, in the mid-1980s, after I took the post of university librarian at Duke University, she volunteered to take over management of our personal affairs. Until that time, she had been an elementary school teacher and during my graduate school days was the primary breadwinner. During the same time, part of my contribution to the marriage was to take care of most of our personal affairs. Seeing the job demands on my time grow at Duke, Veta proposed that she retire from teaching and take a larger share of managing our family and household matters. I agreed. In taking over management of our personal affairs, Veta improved the filing system for all of our important papers; she created the passwords and managed electronic payments for our mortgage and bills; and she managed our insurance, health-related, and other personal policies. She knew where everything was stored. To the degree that anticipation and preparation helps, Veta was as ready for my death as one can be, and I was comfortable knowing that her decisions about next steps for her own life would be easier because she knew how I felt about important matters.

Fortunately, as I was attempting to prepare Veta for my death, she also expressed her preferences about death-related matters to me. I learned many things. Most importantly, I discovered she had almost a phobia about ventilators and was adamant that I never let her be kept on a ventilator long-term. Each time I updated my DNR, she would prepare her own, making sure to reiterate her preference. I learned that she also disliked the thought of me living alone and indicated that if she should die her preference would be for me to find a new companion. In addition, because she did not enjoy open casket viewing or graveside ceremonies common to many of the funerals we attended over the years, she decided that her wish was to be cremated and to have a simple memorial service. Indeed, over the years she revealed and I learned her thoughts and preferences with regard to a wide range of ultimate matters. Thus it happened that while I was preparing Veta for my death, she also prepared me for hers.

The Unthinkable

I may have been prepared for her death in a variety of ways, but that is not to say that I was ready to lose her. That Veta would die was simply unthinkable.

In early December 2009, as we were leaving on a business trip, Veta slipped on a rug in our kitchen, fell, and broke her ankle. It was a bad break of both bones and required surgery. The surgery and her subsequent recovery went well until she had the cast removed and began physical therapy. During the physical therapy, she contracted a bacterial infection on the ankle as it was healing.

The bacteria were identified and a particular antibiotic was prescribed. While she was undergoing treatment for the infection, Veta suddenly began to have difficulty breathing. On two occasions, we took her to the emergency room. The second time, she was admitted to the hospital and treated for pneumonia. When she was released, she was sent home on oxygen to assist her breathing. Soon, however, even with the oxygen she began to have enough difficulty breathing that we returned to the emergency room.

Within twenty-four hours, Veta's breathing had become so labored that she had to be placed on a ventilator. Her worst nightmare had quickly become a reality.

For three weeks the doctors worked without success to solve her problems. As it turned out, the antibiotic that she was taking for her infected ankle sometimes has the side effect of causing lung congestion. Because of the sarcoidosis, the lung congestion quickly turned into both viral and bacterial pneumonias. The only treatment for sarcoidosis was to administer steroids. The steroids, however, suppressed the immune system, which allowed the viral pneumonia to spiral out of control. In the end, she simply could not recover from double pneumonia combined with her pulmonary fibrosis. On April 19, 2010, at 6:50 in the evening, the unthinkable happened: Veta died. The official cause of her death was listed as *adult respiratory distress syndrome* (ARDS).

I will be forever grateful that in the course of our conversations, Veta had always been crystal clear that she did not want to be permanently dependent on a ventilator. She made me promise that I would not allow her to be placed in that situation. In the weeks leading up to the open-heart surgery that I underwent in 2004, she joined me in updating her durable power of attorney, her advance directives, and her DNR order. Because Veta was no longer conscious, when the doctors told me that there was no chance that her lungs would recover sufficiently for her to breathe on her own, I consulted with my daughter (who also knew her mother's wishes) and put the DNR order into effect. Even knowing it was her clear preference, I had never before, nor have I since, experienced anything so gut-wrenching as authorizing Veta's removal from the ventilator and DNR order.

Awareness of Mortality

Our conversations about ultimate things were important for another reason: they gave us an awareness of our own mortality. Though this may seem such an obvious point, I believe it is easy to miss or even avoid such awareness. It is so tempting to go through life and pursue our relationships as if we will live forever, never stopping to contemplate our own mortality, the mortality of those we love, and the implications of mortality for how we live. As a result, we often don't have either our business or personal affairs in order. We leave important things unsaid; we take our loved ones for granted and often fail to express our feelings to them; we clutter our worlds with loose ends. Then when the doctor tells us that we have cancer, we are shocked and stunned suddenly to be faced with the reality that we will die, that we have so little time left, and that we have left so much unsaid and undone.

In the spring of 1967, it became clear that I would need a second heart surgery. The good news was that a workable prosthesis for my problem had been developed. Both Veta and I were twenty-two years old and engaged. Slightly more than six months before we were married, therefore, we had several deep conversations about life and death. As a result, we agreed on a few life and relationship changing matters. They included:

- We pledged that we would never let a day pass without expressing our love for one another.
- We made a pact that we would not allow any disagreement or fight to last more than a day.
- We agreed that we would consciously enjoy one another's company with or without conversation whether working, playing, worshiping, or just relaxing together.

- We decided that we would proactively seek to resolve any difficulties that might arise between us and any family members or friends.
- And we agreed that we should continuously endeavor to keep our personal affairs in order and up to date.

We should, we agreed, without being morbid about it, live as if each day might be our last. And while we did not perfectly live up to our agreement, we came pretty close as these five points of agreement worked their way deeply into our lives. It didn't hurt that our agreement was also periodically refreshed by my recurring heart surgeries.

Though it might seem paradoxical, not only was being aware of our mortality not morbid, it produced some extremely positive outcomes. Even with the usual tribulations of married life, our relationship was relatively trouble-free and the problems short-lived. We enjoyed each other. Perhaps most importantly, we never failed to know of the other's love. And since I had come to be quite comfortable accepting my own mortality and knowing that I was ready if death came my way, it was somehow intellectually easier for me to accept the idea that death would come for Veta as well. My attitude had come to be that my life had been good; if I died that night I would not have been cheated. Though I had to work through the grief process after her death, having talked to her about her death somehow helped me to affirm the same for Veta; her life had been good, and if she died she would not have been cheated in her death.

I am convinced that failure to entertain honestly and accept the inevitability of the death of our loved ones and ourselves is one of the reasons that makes it so difficult for people to deal with death when it comes. It also causes us to think of death as tragedy. If death equals tragedy, then each of us is headed for a tragic end—a conclusion that I reject. It also causes us to fear death and struggle to avoid it. I can attest that having talked deeply and often about death with Veta shaped my view on these matters in a way that allowed me to accept death as a natural, if final, feature of our lives. As a result, even in the grip of my deepest grief I could not think of her death as tragic, and I believe it helped me more quickly to think of her death as the end of a life well lived.

Nonetheless, my grief at her sudden loss was deep and painful.

Personal and Professional Disruption

Veta's mother and her aunt who died as I was writing this both lived till their mid-nineties. Thus I had reason to hope for the same generous lifespan for her. Her sudden death, therefore, was a total surprise that I experienced as traumatic, disorienting, and numbing.

Though I had gone through the deaths of my parents, I had never felt anything like the loss of Veta. As traumatic as it was to lose my parents, I somehow experienced their loss as natural, something to be expected. In this case, I had lost my life-mate. Moreover, Veta was still relatively young, so her death came out of left field. It was triggered by an accident and thus was unexpected.

This did not feel natural. After forty-two years and four months of married life, I suddenly went home to an empty house. The emptiness triggered a viscerally raw sense of loss. The world had lost a beautiful and loving person, someone whose actions actually made the world a better place. If this weren't enough, I was painfully aware of the magnitude of my personal loss. Our interpersonal habits, our customs, our intimacies developed and enjoyed over all those years would be void. Whatever the future held, life would be forever different.

It was immediately and painfully clear to me that not only was Veta gone, her absence would also disrupt every aspect of my personal life. I became aware that grief involved a combination of sorrow over the loss of this wonderful human being and the struggle to deal with the implications of the loss for my life—its impact on daily reality for me. In addition, it was equally clear to me that the disruption brought on by her death would inevitably spill over to my work, degrading the character of my presence, diminishing the quality of my performance, and potentially harming the institution for which I was responsible.

Indeed, many if not most of us have institutional roles that make it difficult for us to take time out to grieve, to go through the grief work necessary to regain some sense of equilibrium in our disrupted lives. While I vowed to work hard to recover from Veta's death, I was aware that, in the wake of a major loss, it takes months or even years to feel whole again.

Thus, the question I faced when Veta died is a question faced by all working individuals in a similar situation. When confronted with such an overwhelming personal disaster, how can I maintain the required professional presence and still carry out my own natural and necessary grief process?

For two days after Veta's death, I found myself groping for a way to answer this question. I managed to do the necessary tasks—arranging for her cremation, calling family and friends, notifying various agencies, and falling apart each evening. By the end of the second day, it was clear to me that muddling chaotically through such tremendous grief as it came would not create a sufficiently dependable way for me both to grieve and to carry on with my work. Muddling through was not a good solution.

I felt a clear, even desperate need for a tool or structure that would allow me to some degree to compartmentalize my personal life from my professional life so that I could give adequate attention to both. I needed a way to manage my grief and maintain at least a modicum of self-control.

Unfortunately, I did not know of such a tool or structure.

Chapter 4: Planning Grief

Once I had ev'ry reason a man could want
For goin' home and makin' love, but now I don't …
Got no reason now for goin' home;
All my reason's now she is gone.[*]

Choosing a Book for a Guide

Because many years earlier in my theological education I had read Elizabeth Kübler-Ross's classic *On Death and Dying*, I had also been interested to read her more recent and final book, *Grief*, co-authored by David Kessler. Since counseling is not my specialty, it is the only book on the subject with which I was familiar. I had even recommended it a few times to friends wanting or needing to understand better the process of grief and grieving.

In the book, Kübler-Ross and Kessler view the grief process through the lenses of five *stages*. Though each of us who experiences grief does so in our own distinctive and individual way, the five stages are intended to function as tools to help us frame and identify what we may be feeling (*Grief*, 7). The stages are: denial, anger, bargaining, depression, and acceptance.

---

[*]   "Got No Reason Now for Goin' Home"; Johnny Russell; recorded by Gene Watson in 1984.

Since I work in academia, I knew that this categorization into stages (first introduced in *On Death and Dying*) has been debated, criticized, and disputed; discussion is one of the ways that learning and understanding progress. Indeed, chapter 1 of *Grief* begins by referring to how the stages have been misunderstood (*Grief*, 7). My goal, however, was not to join the academic debate. I was driven by the urgent need to find a means of creating a grief process for myself that would allow me to maintain a necessary professional presence while also allowing me fully to grieve and emotionally recover from the sudden loss of Veta.

I also had reason to know that the stages of grief could be used to focus and condense grieving in a way that gives it expression but limits its disruptiveness. Indeed, I had used the similar stages outlined in *On Death and Dying* almost twenty-five years ago with the assistance of experts to lead a group of librarians in a workshop we dubbed *Aftershock*. The purpose of the workshop was to help guide the librarians through the shock of major institutional change (the "loss" of old ways of working) and to do so in three days. Aftershock was quite successful, serving to limit organizational malaise and create a more self-aware group of workers.

In this case, it was I who needed an Aftershock guide, but in the form of an intensely personal and flexible guide that could be adapted to an already demanding schedule. I saw no merit in allowing the grief process simply to run thoughtlessly amuck through my life. I was urgently in need of a clear and deliberate means of managing it to some degree. Since I needed a sound mechanism with which to work, knew of none better, and had had the positive experience with the Aftershock workshop, I quickly decided on using the five stages of loss from *Grief* as a guide. And, anyway, I had neither the heart nor time under the circumstances to perform an extended search for some other means of dealing with the quickly building onslaught of grief.

Thus, on the evening of the third day after Veta's death, the end of the first day I returned to work, I sat down with Kübler-Ross and Kessler's five stages to review them as the foundation for creating the guide I needed. Because circumstances did not leave me time to undertake a sophisticated effort to develop a guide based on the book, and since I was rapidly descending into grief, I decided simply to apply the five stages of loss to my already increasingly populated calendar for the coming months.

To put it simply, I built the five-stage grieving process into my schedule.

By doing so, I could insure that I fulfilled my professional responsibilities while scheduling adequate time for grief work. I hoped that neither would be shortchanged.

I also decided that as I worked on a grief process, I would use some principles that had proven useful to me during my health challenges:

- Maintain a high level of self-awareness and intentionality;
- Apply all the spiritual, psychological, and physical resources that had helped me survive multiple open-heart surgeries;
- Let friends and family help as much as possible;
- Be attentive to the needs of others who are also grieving Veta's loss;
- Treat grieving as part of my job and when it is on the calendar give it my undivided attention;
- And set a calendar goal for being back to normal.

To assist me, I decided that I would also develop and pursue a therapy reading list to supplement the Kübler-Ross and Kessler volume as I went along. I felt as if I could use all the help I could get from any source, and so I included solid materials that I had found available on the Internet. This reading list became important as a source for my Saturday morning reading sessions.

Thus, with *Grief* and my calendar, I planned a deliberate season of grief. My goal was to set up a period of time during which I would purposefully use the five stages (undergirded by my own principles and experience) as guides to help myself move through a grief process. I was fully aware of the warnings in the book that the stages were neither "stops on some linear timeline in grief" nor a means to "tuck messy emotions into neat packages" (*Grief,* 7). Though this suggested that grief could not be controlled, I was convinced that it could at least be constructively managed by means of appropriate self-awareness, a suitable guide, and intentionality.

Guidebook for Grieving: Integrating the Stages with the Calendar

I did not know how a guidebook for grieving should be constructed other than to know that it would have to take account of the stages over time. I did know, however, that if I was going to be able to maintain my composure and official demeanor in certain, primarily work-related circumstances, I would need to know that I would have dependable times when I could let down and lose composure. I also knew that I have a tendency to get wrapped up in my work and that doing so could lead me to avoid healthy grieving altogether. Obviously I could alternate between work and home, between public day activities and private time at night, and sometimes this would suffice. It seemed to me, however, that it might require more time than nights and weekends for some of the grieving characterized in the stages to have a healing effect. Plus, I wanted to be sure that I fully experienced and constructively moved through the feelings represented in each of the stages in whatever ways the stages might manifest themselves to me.

While I wanted to assure adequate time for grieving, I did not want the grief process to drag on, so I decided that I would project a deadline for getting through each of the stages. Knowing my own propensity for getting on with life as demonstrated by how quickly I got back to work after my heart surgeries, I decided not to let any of the stages linger—if possible. I would, therefore, set aggressive dates to challenge myself to stay engaged in the grief process and to progress through it. I determined that my return from spending the Christmas and New Year's holidays in North Carolina on January 2, 2011, would be the target date for completing the five stages of the grief process.

I was aware from reading *Grief,* as well as from my own experiences resulting from the deaths of my parents, that feelings associated with the stages would likely recur randomly and out of order. Thus, I knew to take whatever grief calendar resulted from my effort with a large grain of salt. A calendar was simply a guide to add structure and set soft deadlines, to help me be aware of my feelings, and to prevent me from skipping important aspects of my grief work—a structure, not a stricture. If I deviated from the time allotted for any of the stages or if I failed to finish by January 2, 2011, I could simply adjust the calendar with no harm done.

In the end, I decided that as my guidebook the grief calendar could help me achieve three important goals.

- *To allow me to focus on each of the stages.* During the time allotted, I would be deliberate about exploring what I was feeling and in considering what, if anything, I could or should do about it. Thus, the calendar would function both to make certain that I didn't skip or miss something important and to allow me to deal seriously with each of the grief-related emotions that welled up within me. In retrospect, I don't think missing something needs to be too much of a worry, since grief-related feelings and emotions arrive on their own, whether invited or not. When uninvited, however, they may not be dealt with in a healthy, self-aware way, and this may result in problems over time. By making a time to focus on each feeling, I intended to lessen the chance that work demands would inadvertently displace important parts of my grief work.
- *To give me a way to condense grieving time by making it the focus of my attention for concentrated periods.* I made the assumption that reserving specific and private times for expressing my feelings of grief and letting down emotionally could help me move through my experience of the stages more deliberately and quickly. Whether I needed to sob uncontrollably, rant, or simply talk with family or friends, I would create the possibility of doing so at scheduled intervals (such as the already busy work calendar would allow). In this way, the calendar would ensure time for me to express the most intense grief-related feelings and, therefore, get value from them or just get them out of my system. Equally importantly, like post-hypnotic suggestions, the schedule would serve as a guide to prompt me to keep moving through the stages. I would not be left wandering aimlessly through

my grief without a framework for understanding what was happening to me emotionally; the grief process would be focused and not allowed to drag out. I would not get stuck in one of the stages.

- *To give me as much as possible a structure for grieving privately so that I would have a better likelihood of functioning well in public.* It would do so by scheduling grieving into private times when it could be effective for me without being highly disruptive to my demeanor in the workplace; it would give me a tool to compartmentalize grief relative to the private and public parts of my life.

I also decided that I would begin each scheduled stage by rereading relevant portions of Kübler-Ross and Kessler's book along with any other pertinent materials I might find from the list reading I would develop along the way. Thus equipped with the stages, my own rules, a number of obligations for both work and vacation already known, and these goals, I constructed the following simple, sometimes overlapping schedule for grieving.

Creating a Grief Calendar

- Veta's death, April 19, 2010
- *Denial:* April 20—June 30 (End time later changed to June 7, after second memorial service in Lubbock, Texas.)
- *Anger:* June—July (Beginning later changed to June 8.)
- *Bargaining:* July—August (Lasted only two days—not a significant part of my grieving, but very important for an aspect of my self-understanding.)
- *Depression:* September—October (Beginning later changed to early August.)

- *Acceptance:* November—January 2

Week by week, and particularly as each stage approached, I would sit down with a calendar in book form and add detail to this summary, deliberately scheduling specific times (evenings, weekends, and vacation days) to think about and explore how each stage was affecting me. I can't show you that annotated calendar because it and the many details were subsequently lost in a fire described later. The bullet list above is what I outlined just to get started. I recommend annotating the calendar as you go along, because until mine was lost, I found it extremely helpful in monitoring my progress. Indeed, in retrospect, I recommend keeping a journal to document your experience in whatever detail you might wish. Both calendar and journal can be digital.

CHAPTER 5: DENIAL AND THE CHOICE

I don't pick up the mail;
I don't pick up the phone;
I don't answer the door;
I'd just as soon be alone.*

Denial (Disbelief)

While I had built the calendar for grief to emphasize times when I could be away from the office for longer periods, no such opportunity was quickly available, and I knew that the first stage of grief—denial—was already upon me in earnest. My first effort, therefore, was to work with the necessity of grieving during the evenings and on weekends while maintaining my composure during the day at work. I also hoped that maintaining something of a typical schedule would be helpful by providing me with the reliability of a work routine and a reminder that life was going on.

Though I did not go to my office the first two days after Veta died, I did go in on the third day—Thursday. I had plenty to do from the work that had accumulated during the previous three weeks of Veta's hospitalization, but I also spent a couple

---

* "Ghost in This House"; Hugh Prestwood; recorded by Shenandoah, September 20, 1990.

of hours toward the end of the day thinking about my situation. So far, I felt that I was doing okay.

Not until I got home from work that first time did it hit me. The experience of coming home from work where everyone was in their place to a strangely empty house where Veta was missing triggered in me the most intense feelings associated with the first stage of grief—denial.

Throughout Veta's three-week hospitalization, I had company much of the time. My daughter Denise lives only thirty miles away and visited regularly with her friend Sean. My niece Julia had come to stay in our house and help sit with her aunt Veta. My daughter's longtime friend, Abby, and her new husband, Jason, were also frequently with me. Some of Veta's close friends came even though they were not always allowed to enter the intensive care unit. When Veta died, everyone went home. They, too, had to work and grieve.

For me, denial came in the form of disbelief, just as the book described (*Grief*, 8–11). For years I had understood that Veta would eventually die, and intellectually, I had long since accepted the fact of her death as inevitable—though always assuming that I would be the first to go. But accepting something intellectually is vastly different from experiencing the impact of it as a reality. That happened on Thursday. I arrived home from work as usual. Everything looked the same; everything was in its place, but she was not there. I walked through the empty, quiet house and tried to get my feelings adjusted to the fact that she would never return. That's when it hit me emotionally like a ton of bricks.

Veta was gone.

Every aspect of our home bore Veta's distinct imprints of taste and character. Everything cried out to me that she was still here: her cosmetics on the counter, her shoes by the bed, her clothes in the closet, her scent in the rooms. I struggled to maintain my grasp on the reality that she was gone—and that she would not be coming back. I found her absence unbelievable every time I walked in the door or through the house.

That Thursday evening, I outlined the grief calendar.

Friday was the same. I went to work and returned home to an empty house in the evening with an overwhelming sense of disbelief. And there were other triggers for disbelief. Finally, I was recovering my appetite, and it dawned on me that there was literally no fresh food in the house. Since Veta had been in the hospital for almost three weeks and before that was in a wheelchair to keep off her ankle, no one had been grocery shopping. I had eaten everything—or let it spoil. While Veta was in the hospital, I had often eaten in the hospital dining room or in nearby restaurants. During that time, several evening meals had also been prepared by my daughter's friend Sean. Now that family had gone, not only was there no one to greet me when I came home, there was no dinner waiting, no one to ask over a meal how my day had been, no one with whom to talk about the day over a glass of wine. And no food for me to prepare.

Neither would the mail take care of itself; I found the mailbox full. It was quickly stacking up. Veta was widely known and loved, and the first of what would be hundreds of sympathy cards were beginning to arrive. Bills were also in the growing stack. And as if to emphasize her departure, the homeowners' association notified me that day that I would be fined if the trees were not trimmed. Who on earth trimmed our trees? It was one of the myriad things that Veta took care of each year. Time and time again with each new issue that hit, I was struck by disbelief. I realized that the situation would not change until I found a way forward; it would only intensify.

Alone and flooded with such feelings, I poured myself a glass of wine (something that Veta would typically have done for me) and sat down to think. We didn't have wine every night, but we did occasionally, especially when I got home from work and we wanted to sit quietly and talk before dinner. As I sat and pondered, it suddenly hit me that sometime, somewhere I had encountered the statement that one sign of an alcoholic was that the drinker drinks when alone. Though I found some grim humor in the thought, it immediately occurred to me that I actually put myself in a precarious situation by drinking alone in my current state of mind.

Veta's absence changed everything. While my sudden change of circumstances did not mark me as an alcoholic, I knew clearly that without Veta there to talk and make a single drink a part of a pleasant conversation and dinner, I would be tempted to pour another and another and another. After further thought, I decided when alone to give myself a two-glass limit, just to be cautious. In retrospect, that was a good decision. The temptation to drink away the burden of missing Veta was compelling on more than one occasion, especially when the stage marked by depression hit me, and it took considerable willpower to remember my limit and stick with it.

Though the moment with the glass of wine focused me on that issue for a few minutes, I quickly returned to the main subject: how to move forward in the midst of my shock and disbelief over Veta's death and the malaise it cast upon me. Veta died on Monday; it was only Friday. As the first weekend began, it was time for a serious effort at assessing my location on the grief journey that had been thrust upon me.

Choosing to Live

Was life worth living without Veta?

As I examined the feelings of disbelief described above, I realized that this first phase of grief held an oddly tempting danger, that of being overcome and slipping into a personal emotional shell. I could easily see myself deciding just to give up. I could retire and drop out of sight. Who could blame me? In addition, I realized that there was another, more selfish concern mixed up with denial: it was self-pity. With this flipside of denial I had turned inward, concerned with how I could cope with all the implications of Veta's absence, indeed, how I could survive without her. Not only was Veta gone; I was alone. Simultaneously missing someone and feeling the impact of being alone is a powerfully negative combination of feelings. The prospect of life without Veta was more than daunting.

The Broken Heart Syndrome. As I pondered my situation, I recalled reading something about an increased incidence of death among surviving widows and widowers within the first six months after the death of their wife or husband. To confirm my memory, I googled the topic and, indeed, found quite a number of articles that report such a finding based on a variety of sophisticated studies. I was, I then knew, in danger of dying from what is often dubbed the *broken heart syndrome*. I could feel the truth of it. Coincidentally, as if to reinforce the impact of the conclusion reached by the various studies, one of my dear sisters-in-law told me on the phone that I must take care of myself because she had read of this same phenomenon of increased risk of death in persons left behind by the death of their spouses.

How real was this danger for me?

Very real, given the way I felt. I felt almost as if I along with

Veta had also disappeared. I felt inconsequential, insubstantial, like I was not fully there. Veta had always cared about me; had always wanted to know how I was when I traveled; had always waited for my text messages and phone calls. She had always greeted me when I came home. At every moment of the day or night, I knew that someone cared for me in a special way. Of course my family and friends still cared, but not with the same intense interest of a life-mate who focused on me. Suddenly no one similarly focused on me was there. As a result, I felt invisible, transparent, and numb. It didn't matter where I was or whether I got there safely; it didn't matter when or whether I came home after work; no one knew or cared. The one to whom it had mattered was gone. I could understand how easy it would be to drop out of life, to go into hermit mode.

Such feelings also caused me to realize how much my identity and self-understanding depended on Veta after forty-three years of living together. Much of my own sense of self and self-definition was derived from the relationship between Veta and me. We had habits of relating to one another that made us a successful couple for many years. These habits of relating included intimate and thorough knowledge of one another that was built on shared experiences and being side by side through everything life threw at us. It was as if Veta's intimate knowledge of who I was functioned as a force to help me remain who I was, to remain me. Her very presence exerted expectations on the content and character of *me*. There were things about me that only she knew. When she died, that part of me was no longer sustained by her knowledge and expectations. It seemed as if at least part of who I was had already died with her.

Then there was the practical side of things. I suddenly came face-to-face with the magnitude of work previously handled by Veta that would now fall to me. It was initially overwhelming.

This work obviously included taking care of such basic matters as food, laundry, taxes, and finances, as well as keeping up house and yard. It would necessarily impact my functioning as a president of a school by limiting the time, both day and night, that I could spend working. Regardless of whether I ended up hiring others to help me, I would simply have to devote more of my time to non-work-related personal necessities.

Worst of all, of course, was the loss of Veta herself—the person about whom I cared most passionately and intensely, my wife of many wonderful years; the person who had shared everything with me, good times and bad, joy and sorrow; the person who had depended upon me and upon whom I had depended. Her absence was disorienting, and her death was agonizing and unbelievable. It seemed that all I could do when alone was weep. The world had lost a wonderful, kind, and caring human being, and I had lost my wife and best friend.

Loneliness. And then there was the loneliness. I was alone for the first time in my almost sixty-five years. I was raised in an extended family that consisted of my father and mother, aunt Mary, and uncles John and Albert. I never had a babysitter. In addition, I had two brothers and a sister. It is difficult to be alone in such a household. In college, I had a roommate and two suite mates. Halfway through my senior year of college, Veta and I married. Living alone, therefore, had not been a significant part of my childhood or adult experience.

On the other hand, I did enjoy solitude and often arranged purposefully to be by myself. This included occasional retreats where I was deliberately by myself for periods of time, usually varying from a day to a week. Until I graduated from college, these personal retreats took place mainly on the Campbell family ranch in Northwest Texas ranch country. Later I would also go to the mountains of Colorado or North Carolina or to the deserts of New Mexico or Arizona. I needed the solitude and found it greatly restorative for mind, body, and spirit. Veta enjoyed such times as well and occasionally went on retreats of her own. Retreats, however, are by arrangement and are limited in duration. They are decidedly unlike living alone.

In the midst of these thoughts, I remembered and found in my personal library a short book written and given to me thirty-five years ago by a now deceased pastor, theologian, and friend, Harvey H. Potthof, entitled *Loneliness: Understanding and Dealing With It* (Nashville: Abingdon, 1976). I reread it.

Harvey's perspective in *Loneliness* was very helpful to me. He wrote: "It is almost certain that loneliness will be experienced in the later years. But what that loneliness comes to mean to us is partly our own decision." (*Loneliness*, 47) He further observed:

> What has been done has been done. The experiences we have had with parents and family, the fortunate and unfortunate relationships we have experienced, the successes and failures which have been part of our lives, the joys and sorrows we have known, are in the lived record and cannot be changed.
>
> What can be changed is the meaning these events and experiences have for us. If we wish, we can make a lifelong career of living in the past. We can make some past misfortune or injustice the focal point of our thinking and living. On the other hand, we can draw rich treasures from the past, learn from what we have experienced, and go on to new chapters of life. We are given the gift of life one day at a

time and each new day is a new gift. (*Loneliness*, 53–54)

Though I simply could not yet even think about new chapters of life, Harvey's perspective helped me realize that if I could change my perspective—see my own situation, my being alone, in a different way, I would at least create the possibility of reducing the pain of being alone. In the best-case scenario, I might even begin to derive some value from my time alone and find some growth as a result of Veta's death. It was at the time seemingly impossible, but I could hold it as a hope, a possibility.

As I pondered this, it occurred to me that among other things, my situation would provide me with an opportunity (unwanted though it was) to more fully explore the potential benefits of solitude. Recalling how much I enjoyed occasional solitude, I knew that I needed to make a conscious effort to shift my point of view. I needed to stop thinking of my circumstance as debilitating loneliness and conceive of it as restorative solitude, to think of my situation as that of being in a new era of plentiful solitude as opposed to being left alone.

I was aware that this would not suddenly remove the feelings brought about by Veta's absence, but it would give me a way to begin to put a positive element in my feelings about the situation.

As I sorted out the matter of being alone, I also realized that most of the large assortment of friends I had enjoyed had resulted from Veta's efforts to nurture the social aspect of our life together. The result, I knew, would be that I would not be good at nurturing these relationships, and I surmised that these couple-based friends would be less likely to be as comfortable with me alone. Though there would be notable exceptions, in general, this proved to be true as time went on.

Similarly, I anticipated that the status of my role as president would prevent work colleagues from reaching out as friends beyond the workplace. And again with notable exceptions, this proved to be the case. It was clear, therefore, that most of my time outside the workplace would be spent alone unless I expended the energy and effort deliberately to nurture existing or develop new friendships. It was also clear that the demands of my role as president, the physical limits on my energy, and my somewhat introverted character meant that I should get accustomed to being alone.

I knew, of course, that great numbers of people live alone. Of these, many do so by choice, but others do so out of necessity. When it is out of necessity and when it is thrust upon one suddenly, it is a jolt to the system that takes some getting used to—even if one appreciates, even enjoys, solitude.

I sat there as that first weekend approached and thought about how to deal with these feelings. Since I was just beginning my journey into grief, I decided that there were two things I had to do if I was going to give myself the chance to adjust emotionally. The first was practical and straightforward: I could get busy and clean up all the tasks stacking up. The second was more complicated and required me to make a decision that would be difficult in the immediate aftermath of Veta's death. I had to decide whether I wanted to live or give in to the emotional pain and simply let go—whether to become a victim of the broken heart syndrome.

Tackling the Stuff. Starting with the stuff, I began the challenging process of dealing with all the personal matters that Veta had previously handled for us. As I contemplated this action, I was embarrassed when it occurred to me how my horrible new circumstance is everyday fare for countless other individuals. Worse yet were the difficulties faced by single parents. How much more challenging would it be if Denise were still an infant or child? As for me, grief notwithstanding, I could, as the saying goes, "Suck it up," and get busy taking care of the details of my new life alone. And while I was at it, I could quit feeling quite so sorry for myself. This would give me a reality check and refocus some of my energy on daily necessities. These necessities included: taking control of my personal finances (I would find passwords or take steps to have accounts changed to allow new ones); developing at least adequate skills for cooking and otherwise providing for my own care (some of my work colleagues would soon give me a wonderful cooking class); and generally taking responsibility for all matters relating to living and working (including trimming the trees).

The necessities also included proceeding with a variety of arrangements relating to Veta's death. These involved arranging both for certain concrete actions and for more emotional adjustments. As for the actions, someone, I thought, should develop a checklist for nearest of kin in such situations; it was not exactly a time when I was clear-headed. As it turns out, of course, there are such checklists. But at the time, no one recommended one, and I neglected to check Google! Instead, late that Thursday evening (after I drafted the simple grief calendar) I made my own:

1. Finish arrangements relating to cremation (choose urn, decide how many locks of hair, did I want a thumbprint made, etc.);
2. Arrange for death certificates (I got a dozen and should have gotten more.);
3. Make notifications (friends and family, bank, credit card companies, department stores where Veta held

accounts, Social Security Administration, insurance carriers, estate attorney);

4. Notify insurance companies;
5. Change accounts that carried Veta's name;
6. Collaborate with my daughter Denise who had asked to take care of all arrangements for the memorial services;
7. Inventory the refrigerator and pantry (check expiration dates);
8. Arrange for Denise, Julia, and Abby to go through closets, drawers, and dressers;
9. Decide where to donate Veta's clothes, shoes, handbags, and clothing accessories that the family did not want to keep and deliver the items;
10. Decide what to do with (or execute Veta's wishes relative to) certain of her personal items;
11. Make first solo trip to grocery store (make a list first!);
12. Go to Costco and get a carload of tissues.

It was not a complete list, but it was a place to start. Engaging in these concrete actions began quietly to counter my feelings of disbelief. And by inviting Denise, Julia, and Abby in on the process, it would also give them a chance to work on some of their grief as well. Items 7, 8, and 9 were particularly meaningful to them. Julia helped me with the food inventory, and in the process of doing so I began for the first time to think about how I would approach my ongoing need to prepare food. Julia also went with me to Costco, where we purchased food for family and friends coming to the first memorial service and enough boxes of tissues, it seemed, to last a lifetime. As it turned out, I soon found myself picking up more tissues.

Over the weekend, all three young women tackled the closets, drawers, and dressers. Though I remained at home, I left to them the task of removing Veta's clothes and accessories from closets and removing her things from drawers. In doing so, they made wonderfully sensitive decisions, setting aside certain articles for family and friends and bagging the rest to give away. Every article of clothing, every pair of shoes, every handbag brought a flood of memories, and the spirit and manner in which these young women carried out their work was a great gift to me.

Their working through closets and drawers caused me to remember the days following my mother's death when my siblings and our spouses did the same in Dad's home. I thought of him sitting alone quietly in the living room as we went through Mom's things, and only all these years later did I fully know the inner turmoil that belied his stoic outer demeanor. In that circumstance, as the bereft spouse I could not help but feel that parts of me, parts of my life, were being sorted out and readied for discarding, and I am certain that is how Dad felt. The sorting was necessary, but it was not in any way a good feeling. I could consciously recognize the feeling of denial within myself: "This can't be happening. How can they be sorting through Veta's clothes and personal effects?" The situation drove home the fact of Veta's death, but it had not yet become an emotional reality for me just as it had not been for Dad in the aftermath of Mom's death.

Giving Veta's personal clothing and accessories away (I chose a shelter for battered women) was excruciatingly difficult. As providence would have it, while stopping by my office on my way to the shelter, I encountered one of our students, Beth, who perceived my struggle and simply accompanied me and helped unload the clothes. That also was a tremendous gift to me.

As in times of my surgeries, I found that letting others

help was exceedingly beneficial to me, and I hope that it was an equally positive experience for them.

Another major example of such help was Denise's interest in assuming responsibility for her mother's memorial services. Denise and I had agreed that we would have two memorial services: the main service being on May 16 in Pasadena, California, and a second service on June 7 in Lubbock, Texas, for those of Veta's family and friends for whom travel would be difficult. The gap between Veta's death and the first memorial service was set at four weeks so that family and friends scattered throughout the US would have time to make travel plans to attend and so that it would not coincide with the week of commencement at the school where I was serving as president. The memorial services were expertly and sensitively arranged by Denise, who inherited from her mother the marvelous traits of good taste and skills for organizing.

Both services were emotionally intense and important, and Denise's taking responsibility for those services allowed me to focus on Veta's family members and friends in ways that would not have been possible if I had been seeing to the details. More importantly, I believe arranging those services was immensely therapeutic for Denise—a way for her to be intimately involved in the last acts of taking care of her mother.

Thus, I found it immeasurably helpful to take on the "stuff" that had been accumulating. It both gave me something useful to do and began to provide a counterbalance to my disbelief and the corresponding feeling of being inconsequential. It did so by systematically reminding me that the situation was real; Veta had died. And it did so by reassuring me that I could manage my affairs.

The Fundamental Choice. As for the second task, I set aside that first weekend after Veta's death while Denise, Julia, and

Abby sorted clothing to struggle with a fundamental decision about my own life and death. A weekend, however, was not long enough. The struggle stayed with me throughout the following week.

I knew, based on my experience surviving heart surgeries, that it is sometimes necessary to make a conscious decision to live. Heart surgeries, especially those that are complicated and difficult, require not only skilled work on the part of the surgeon and his or her team; they also require a serious determination on the part of the patient to survive. On the occasion of my fifth heart surgery (during Christmas week in 1990), my surgeon said to me, "My team is ready, but this is going to be very complicated. We can only do so much. If you are going to make it through this, you will have to meet me at the fifty yard line." I took that football metaphor to mean that it was at least as much dependent upon my determination and effort as his whether the surgery succeeded.

I felt that this circumstance would also require similar determination. Though the reasons why there is an increased risk of death among surviving widows and widowers appeared not to be well understood ("broken heart" does not seem to me to be a precise medical diagnosis), I was convinced that to some degree it had to do with one's determination to go on living in the midst of overwhelming sadness and sense of loss. One's body responds directly to one's mental and psychological state of mind. For instance, for the first time in years, after Veta's death I had to increase the amount of prescription anticoagulant I took in order to maintain a constant therapeutic result.

Dealing with Veta's death, therefore, was already changing my body chemistry! Since my own history of cardiovascular disease reportedly gave me an even greater risk of death statistically in the next six months (according to one of the reports I read), I would have to make an effort to keep such changes from being detrimental to my well-being. I wondered if I had it in me to muster the will to make such an effort.

I would have to decide with certainty whether I wanted to go on living without Veta.

Ironically, my first inclination was to argue to myself that it was too soon after Veta's death to make such a decision. Another helpful book sent to me shortly after Veta's death by a friend and author Bob Deits (*Life after Loss*, fifth edition, Cambridge, MA, 2009) suggested that survivors like me are in a state of shock (*Loss*, 57). That is exactly how I felt. How could I choose between life and death when I was in shock? I should, I thought, at least wait until I had made it through the grief process to decide; it would clearly be a better, more thoughtful decision at that point. At this stage, I was distraught and in no condition to make such a momentous decision. That is how I felt.

Obviously, I was in a predicament. Even with what I considered to be an aggressive grief calendar, it would take at least eight months to get through the process. If the risk of death for a surviving spouse is greatest in the first six months, then the option of waiting to make such a fundamental decision until my grief had run its course was not a good option. I might die while waiting until a more convenient, reasonable time to make a decision in favor of life.

It was, I realized, not unlike facing the sudden failure of a mechanical heart valve. There was no time to wait and think about the situation until I found a level of comfort with a course of action. There was only an immediate choice between surgery and a chance for life or no surgery and certain death. Though a broken heart is less tangible than a broken prosthesis, my heavy sadness, the reports of the statistical likelihood of my death as a surviving spouse, and my own forebodings are all I had with which to make a decision.

It was not a good or convenient or comfortable time to decide between life and death, but it was precisely the time when the choice had to be made.

I took the thought that I could not go on living without Veta and turned it over in my mind. I explored it, probed it. My love for her and my commitment to her made the thought of my own death plausible, even compelling. My own letting go in the aftermath of her unexpected death would stand as a demonstration of the deep substance of that love and commitment. And anyway, I was suffering from the shock of it and simply didn't know if I could muster all the energy necessary to keep from finally relaxing the intentional grip on life that my medical history had required. Yes—that I could let go was quite plausible.

The possibility of letting go professionally was similar. I had a long, successful, and satisfying career in libraries and technology and had no professional bucket list. I was satisfied on that score. Well, almost. I had moved to Claremont School of Theology in 2006 and had begun to lead a process of institutional change that was not quite finished. It was, however, far enough along that the character of the changes underway was established, and my board, staff, and faculty colleagues were clearly capable of completing the task. I felt that if I let go, the vision would continue unimpeded without me.

Though condensed here, I struggled with these thoughts throughout the weekend as my girls worked through the closets. I could hear them alternately crying and laughing. They were adults now with their own lives. It occurred to me that one of the outcomes I should avoid at all costs was placing a burden on them for my emotional upkeep and well-being. If I decided in favor of life, I would have to learn to be more emotionally dependent upon myself than I had ever been. In addition, if I decided for life, it would have to be because I wanted to live for my sake, not simply for theirs. Their lives were not wrapped up with mine; they were emotionally healthy and strong and would get over losing me if that should be the result of my decision.

My struggle with this decision continued through the following week.

In the final analysis, I concluded, the decision to live is intensely personal. Even if you think it is for the benefit of someone else, you finally decide for yourself. On the second weekend after Veta's death, as I struggled between life and death, I had a sudden insight: I had already decided! I was just sorting through the issues until I became aware of the decision. It occurred to me with almost the impact of an electric shock that the very process of creating a grief calendar in order to manage my grief to a positive outcome was a de facto decision to live. If I had wanted to give up and die, I would not have been concerned about muddling through grief or its potentially debilitating effect on my performance on the job. I would have simply defaulted: Forget the inner turmoil and struggle. I've lost Veta; I've lost the will to live; I'm letting go.

But no, I had already chosen life; I just had not recognized it.

Albeit through tears, I laughed at myself. I believe that throughout all those heart surgeries, I had developed a tremendous will to live. Even though I had told myself it was because I needed to survive to provide for my family (and there was truth in that), the multiple occasions had created within me an almost habitual determination to survive. It had, I realized, kicked in unconsciously. Subconsciously I was already preparing to live; I had just then become consciously aware of it. In addition, my old departed friend Harvey's book had given me a start on using my aloneness as an opportunity and means to enrich my spiritual life. I could now pursue what are often referred to as *spiritual disciplines* to a new and deeper level.

Previously I noted that much of my identity was based on who Veta knew me to be. When someone else (a spouse, significant other, parents, or children) knows us so intimately, that person's knowledge and expectations of us help hold us in place—keep us being who we are. This can be a good or bad thing, reinforce positive or negative habits, keep us out of trouble, or get us continually into trouble. For this reason, the last great gift a departed loved one gives us is the freedom to make life changes; that intimate knowledge of who we are departs with them. We become free to consider, even reconsider, who we are and make adjustments, to change and grow. Though it was a bitter loss, I would also try to understand that in her going, Veta had given me a last extraordinary gift: a rare unqualified opportunity for clarifying my values and more fully embodying them in my actions.

I was faced, therefore, with how to go forward in a way that favored life and personal growth. I thought that for starters I could make a conscious decision to refuse to give in to the numbness, the feeling of being inconsequential as a result of Veta's death, and to be alert to the fact that I now had the sole responsibility for who I am. I would also, I decided, begin to do more work with the spiritual disciplines as a means of converting loneliness into the more satisfying notion of solitude.

My experience surviving surgeries also helped me move forward with this opportunity for values clarification. This was not unlike the situation surrounding such surgeries. Those surgeries were so complicated that it was never clear whether I would survive. As I approached them, therefore, I recognized that if I did survive, I had the opportunity to put away those things I did not wish to continue in order to become someone new and better. And afterward, I had the challenge of following through with the life changes that I had decided would be desirable. In her dying, Veta, with whom I had on several occasions discussed changes I might undertake after my surgeries, had gifted me with a similar challenge and opportunity. Though brought about by a very different, painful, and sad circumstance, here again was another chance to refine my own life.

Because my decision to live raised a corollary question of what I might do about entering a new relationship, and because it really was too early to decide this matter, I determined that if asked, I would respond to this subject by simply saying that I had no plans to develop another relationship. I relate this only because quite a number of people who cared for me—family and friends—began asking me almost immediately about my plans in that regard. Since I had not even tried to take on that question, it was a helpful (and truthful) response that I used quite a number of times over the next several months.

By the end of that difficult weekend, I consciously confirmed the decision: I wanted to live and would do all that I could to avoid being numbered among the statistics of those who died quickly as a result of the death of their beloved spouse.

Moving Past Disbelief

As noted earlier, the memorial services were intense and important. At the first memorial, the intensity was, in part, simply a function of sitting with hundreds of friends and family and paying tribute to Veta's remarkable life and influence. After the service, my immediate family and I stood in a receiving line for two and a half hours, greeting and thanking those who attended. Perhaps there is an explanation of why it helps to come together in this way with friends and family to acknowledge someone's passing, but I can only attest to the fact that it did help and that it was a notable early marker on the pathway to accommodating emotionally the difficult truth of Veta's death. It helped me sufficiently that in my subsequent reflections I decided that the Lubbock memorial service should be the marker after which I would move to the second stage, anger.

A month later, on June 7, 2010, the second memorial service in Lubbock was different but equally meaningful. It was attended by a much smaller gathering of close family and friends and was held in a family member's home. It was a more intimate, emotionally charged event with sensitive and appropriate remarks by a clergyman who was married to one of Veta's relatives. Acknowledging Veta's death with her family also underlined the reality and finality of her death. On my way back to California, I felt as if I was no longer experiencing the intense denial that gripped me in the immediate aftermath of her death; I had begun to come to terms with the fact that Veta was gone, not to return.

The somewhat artificial time limit on denial had been effective. I not only felt as if I could now walk into my Upland home without the numbing feeling of disbelief, I also realized with some surprise that I was already experiencing the kind of anger associated with stage two.

Chapter 6: Anger

You don't know who I am,
But I know all about you ...
Let me introduce myself:
I am the cold hard truth.[*]

Feeling Angry

I am by practice and personal ethics not given to emotional extremes, so the *anger* caught me off guard. I have worked consciously throughout my adult life not to be overcome by anger because it violates my deepest conviction about how humans should respond to one another. In my case, however, the conscious practice of remaining calm during emotionally charged moments long preceded the development of my ethical preference.

I was told after my first heart surgery at the age of thirteen to avoid emotional extremes because of the stress it puts on my cardiovascular system. So serious was my cardiologist about this that he instructed my father to sit near me at hometown football games to make sure that I did not jump and scream when the home team scored. If I did exhibit such outbursts, he

---

[*] "The Cold Hard Truth", Jamie O'Hara, recorded by George Jones in 1999.

advised my father to take me home and no longer allow me to go to the games. For me this would have been a severe penalty, not so much because I would miss football, but because I would miss my absolutely favorite endeavor—playing in the band. The threat of missing band was enough to instill within me a keen focus on staying calm—even during the most exciting moments.

Thus it was that I learned to think about what I was feeling before expressing those feelings. Over time, it became second nature for me to be consciously analytical about my feelings, and as a result, I have rarely exhibited emotional outbursts. The few times I have lost some emotional control, my experience was that allowing myself to feel, certainly to express, excessive anger or excitement had a negative physical impact on my own body. I could literally feel the effect of anger on my own body, and I did not like it. As a result, I practiced avoiding emotional extremes, particularly anger. Anger, therefore, was never a useful tool for me and, for that reason, became increasingly unusual as a feature of my ordinary emotional experience. So it is rare for me to feel and express anger in a way that is observable by those around me.

Nonetheless, as the numbness of denial began to recede, I was feeling angry.

I replayed over and over and over again in my mind the events that led up to Veta's hospitalization and, ultimately, her death. I agonized over why I didn't realize in advance that her sarcoidosis would be such a life-threatening problem for her. I pondered why, when she developed pneumonia, I didn't have the good sense to take her to a large hospital in the area which had a women's lung institute. I wondered why I didn't take her to the hospital sooner. I realized that what I was feeling was anger at myself. I felt responsible for her death.

I also found myself having terrible thoughts about the hospital and her doctors. Why didn't the hospital recognize the seriousness of her situation the first time she was admitted to the emergency room? Were the doctors incompetent, or did they simply not care enough to save her?

In my grief calendar, I had reserved a number of times after the second memorial service to reflect on the transition from denial to anger. It was during one of these times that I was able, with the help of *Grief*, to acknowledge my anger. The short section on anger (*Grief*, 11–17) described me almost perfectly.

In the midst of my anger, it was shocking to be reminded that I was not the first person to have suffered such a terrible loss. This was an obvious and easy fact for me to grasp when not engaged in the grief process. The process of intense grieving, however, created an irrational emotional isolation that caused me to feel as if my tragedy was unmatched, certainly unsurpassed. Just reading from *Grief* gently disabused me of this delusion; just to be reminded that countless human beings before me had been subjected to such loss gave me a perspective from which I could begin to contextualize my feelings.

Nonetheless, I set aside times to let my anger run. I purposely thought the angriest thoughts I was capable of forming; I verbalized my disgust with the medical officials and institutions involved; I was particularly hard on myself. These anger exercises usually ended with the uncomfortable thought that the foundations for the specific, directed anger were illogical and irrational. Thus, paradoxically, at the same time I felt anger, I also felt that it was unfounded, even unfair. What doctor wants to lose an otherwise healthy patient? And the highly rated community hospital could not have wanted to lose Veta or any patient. In fact, I remembered the genuine grief that all her doctors and hospital representatives demonstrated at the time of her death.

Following my grief calendar gave me opportunities to get my anger out, but it also gave me moments of objectivity that assured me that my feelings of anger were normal and okay, as long as I did not get stuck in them. In one moment of reflection, I realized that such feelings, if they lingered, would only serve to traumatize me more and still would not change what had happened. I also began to experience a more self-conscious and manageable way to deal with my feelings of anger directed toward myself, the hospital, and the doctors.

It is remarkable how becoming aware of my anger helped keep it from becoming disruptive when I was in the workplace. The experience reinforced my belief that self-awareness is the key to anger management and that failing to recognize one's own anger might likely lead to a situation in which the anger will come bubbling out unexpectedly and perhaps uncontrollably. Conversely, anger that is examined, recognized, and even expressed privately is less likely to be disruptive in unexpected ways and times. As a result of being self-conscious about my anger, I believe I was able both to experience it in a way that was ultimately healthy and to prevent it from affecting my professional presence to any significant degree. I was also personally more comfortable because this manner of dealing with emotional extremes fit my customary pattern.

As I went through the anger exercises and thought about the anger I had for myself, my guilt finally began to dissipate. Awareness of facts and circumstances eventually overcame the irrationality of guilt: I could not have known more than I did; there was no time to get to a more distant hospital; I did everything possible within my control as quickly as possible. While the sequence of causes was clear in retrospect (Veta's accident, the infection, the antibiotic, the double pneumonia, the sarcoidosis), how they came together to create a fatal circumstance was something that neither I nor the doctors could have anticipated.

Veta's death was no one's *fault*.

While the exercises and reflection significantly eased my anger and guilt at the time, it turned out that they were not sufficient to keep the guilt from affecting me in a more subtle way before the summer was out, so I will return to this subject when I get to the discussion of the stage characterized by depression.

Earlier I indicated that the description of anger in *Grief* "almost" described me. One aspect of anger that I never experienced was anger toward Veta for leaving me. Perhaps it was because I witnessed how hard she struggled to live during her hospitalization. In any case, though I read of it and purposefully spent time thinking about it, that aspect of anger did not materialize as a part of my experience; I did not feel it. This emphasized for me a point made early in *Grief* that while the stages might be generally descriptive, each individual's experience would be unique (7).

As I began to explore my feelings of anger after the second memorial service, and knowing my capacity to manage it, I decided that I would try to be finished with anger at the conclusion of the second of my summer travels. My summer travels included four sets of travel: a personal vacation in North Carolina, a study trip with a group of ten Christians to the Hartman Institute in Israel, a trip to a seminar at an educational and spiritual retreat center in Wyoming, and a week at Chatauqua, New York, for an interreligious program. The first two of these, I decided, would give me adequate personal time to work on my anger.

North Carolina: The Aerie

Looking forward to retirement, Veta and I built a retirement home in southwestern North Carolina in the Smoky Mountains. The house is near that of longtime friends and occupies a location that gives it a magnificent long-range view of layers and layers of mountain ridges. It had become a retreat that we both loved. I could think, write, pray, and meditate while Veta sometimes joined me in prayer and meditation, in addition to her own reading, writing, and just plain relaxing. Because of my lifetime love of raptors and a pair of bald eagles that flew over during my first visit after construction started, I named our retirement home The Aerie.

The arrival of July and the first of my summer travels would give me the first opportunity to return to Aerie since Veta had died, and I knew it would be something of a test to return to the house we had planned and built together for our golden years. If I could deal constructively with my anger in that setting, I thought, I would be well on my way to getting through the anger stage.

On a number of occasions, Veta and I invited two close friends, George and Linda, to join us at the Aerie. They were diligent in calling me during my grief and on one such occasion asked about my summer vacation plans. When I told them I was going to North Carolina with some trepidation, they quickly indicated that they were taking me up on our former invitations and would be joining me. It would be great for them, they indicated, because George might be able to see one of his sons and daughter-in-law, and we might also get in some fly-fishing. George could join me from the outset, and Linda would arrive a few days later.

Though this had not been a part of my plan, I remembered

my rule about letting friends help. So it was with some relief that I welcomed their company; I did not have to return to the Aerie alone.

When I entered the Aerie the first time, even with George at my side, however, I momentarily slipped back into disbelief, being gripped by the sudden sensation that the person who had helped plan the Aerie simply couldn't be gone forever. It was the same sense of disbelief that I had finally gotten over at my home in Upland. Once again I was conscious of the fact that every part of the house, from its basic design to the pottery on the mantle, reminded me of Veta. This was the place we planned together and where we intended to live out our final years together. I suddenly found myself experiencing both disbelief and anger together. This I knew would be a difficult trip.

George somehow knew how, without words, to be appropriately solicitous while giving me plenty of space. At night, I had ample time and opportunity to explore my feelings deeply, sometimes weeping in solitude. For daytime activities, we visited George's son and daughter-in-law, fished, read, and George gave me cooking lessons. Perhaps the most meaningful thing, however, was our work in Veta's flower bed. George is a capable horticulturist, and with his help, the flowerbed she had begun was completed.

When Linda arrived I told them that I intended to gather the clothes that Veta kept at Aerie in order to take them to Goodwill. The two of them invited me to go sit on the deck while they gathered her clothes. I protested weakly but yielded to their suggestion. Without asking they also loaded the clothes in my car and accompanied me to Goodwill.

In retrospect, I realized that their presence and help with Veta's clothes was the greatest gift they could have given me at the time. They lifted a great burden from my shoulders. They offered no advice and uttered no consoling platitudes; they simply stayed by my side and comforted me with their actions. And wisely, they stayed long enough to lend emotional help, but left in time for me to have a few days alone before my return. Their actions were an important healing and learning experience for me, and I will always be grateful to them for their gift.

When they left, I was able to walk through Aerie without disbelief. I was also back to a more self-conscious and managed feeling of anger. I spent the remaining days of my time at Aerie in deep reflection; I was largely over being angry at myself, the doctors, and the hospital. Though the feeling of anger particularly at myself would reappear a few times, usually provoked by circumstances, it would never again have its initial intensity. The results of the anger would, however, play a more subtle and dangerous role a short time later.

Having the Israel trip remaining on my calendar to deal with anger, I was ahead of schedule. For reasons explained below, I had not experienced anger toward God, but since that kind of anger figured prominently in *Grief* I decided to spend the balance of the allocated time focusing on the idea of anger at God and the related matter of the relationship of God and evil.

Anger at God

Up to this point I have addressed only the anger I felt toward myself, the doctors, and the hospital. This leaves what I find to be the most interesting aspect of anger described in *Grief*, that of anger toward God. To oversimplify, the thought that God is responsible for everything including great evil (such as the death of a loved one) often drives us to be angry at God in the most intense situations. I needed to think this through.

Since my college years, it never suited me to think of God in terms associated largely with seventeenth- and eighteenth-century philosophers and theologians from whom some popular contemporary ideas of God derive. Rather, in college I was introduced to a form of theology known as *process theology* (Process). Process is based on the twentieth-century thought of British Philosopher Alfred North Whitehead and was developed by theologians Charles Hartshorn (University of Chicago), John Cobb (Claremont School of Theology), and David Ray Griffin (Claremont School of Theology) among others.

Though Process was at that time still in the early stage of its full articulation, I was drawn to it because it was compatible with my experience of the world. Process easily accommodates the rapid growth of human knowledge and doesn't require that I make untenable choices between explanations of reality associated with antiquated world views and those based on what we have continued to learn through a variety of educational and scientific endeavors. It also obviated such distractions as the futile argument between evolution and creationism. This was significant to me because in the Wesleyan tradition within which I was nurtured, one's experience is an important ingredient (along with Scripture, history, and reason) in making sound judgments both in theological matters and in living out one's discipleship. With Process, it was possible, therefore, for me to adopt a view of God that did not repeatedly come into conflict with my experience of reality or my rationality.

There was another significant reason that Process appealed to me, but I did not become aware of it until I had moved on to the next stage of grief, that of *bargaining*. Thus, I will return to this subject below.

As it turns out, Process also characterizes God in a way that does not invite anger toward God. In Process thought, God is not conceived of as an anthropomorphic figure, a super-person (usually a super*man*), pulling all the strings on events, actions, and outcomes. Rather, God is viewed as an integral part of and the sustaining principle upholding all reality. This *Sustaining Principle* (my label) has persuasive power rather than coercive power and all of creation, though dependent upon the Sustaining Principle for existence, is characterized as having self-determination. God *influences* outcomes, therefore, rather than *determining* outcomes. In other words, God is actively present in all that happens without dictating, manipulating, or being solely responsible for what happens. In effect, this means that neither did God cause Veta's death nor could God have prevented it.

I did not expect, therefore, to experience anger toward God because it was not compatible with the way I think about God. And, indeed, I did not. I nonetheless purposefully thought about God and Veta's death. It was clear to me that if I reverted to thinking of God as I did in my pre-collegiate years, I would necessarily have to assign some of the blame to God. But I simply no longer thought about God that way.

I did, however, experience a great difficulty in praying. During the time of anger toward myself and others, I suddenly realized that I was avoiding my regular habits of prayer. Even after I became conscious of this, I found prayer to be an extremely difficult, almost objectionable endeavor. As I pondered why, I drew the conclusion that my *prayer block* was most likely in the same category as anger at God.

As I pondered why this was so, I decided there were two

possible explanations. In the first place, it might have been that in the stressful circumstances surrounding the loss of Veta, from a psychological view I simply needed to blame something beyond myself, the doctors, and hospital. And my pre-collegiate version of God supplied the handiest target for such blame, especially since that idea of God made God the causal agent of everything. So maybe the inability to pray was a subconscious substitute for consciously blaming God even though it conflicted with my Process orientation. The problem, however, was not that I blamed or felt angry at God; I just couldn't bring myself to pray in the customary way. I concluded that simply needing to blame something larger was not the best explanation.

In the second place, and more likely, I decided my prayer block arose because prayer was the one remaining place in my religious life where I had been willing to accommodate my pre-collegiate understanding of God. Although I had long ago adopted a Process way of thinking about God, I had not fundamentally altered the manner in which I prayed, primarily for practical reasons. It seemed sensible to continue to pray using language and concepts that would be recognized by and comfortable to those with whom I worshipped; no need to raise questions or create problems for others by using a terminology that would be unfamiliar to most of those around me. It would be better, I had decided, for me simply to know the difference.

Though I put this inability to pray in the same category as anger at God, it was not an exact match. Never did I feel anger; it was more that I found expressing prayer in a way that was at odds with my long-held Process view to be inappropriate given the intensity of my feelings. The traditional prayer pattern and language that I learned as a youngster and that are typically used in the churches I frequent do assume in general the concept of God as omnipotent and, therefore, ultimately and directly responsible for everything—including Veta's death.

I had ceased praying, therefore, because praying in the old paradigm implicitly violated my own understanding of God. When this became clear to me during my last few days at the Aerie, I knew that in the short run I certainly could not follow my usual prayer pattern. I decided that I would put prayer on hold until I could find a way forward. As it turned out, I would have to learn another way of praying in order to be able to pray again. It was not until after an experience I had with a Buddhist monk later in the summer that I found another pattern and recovered the ability to pray.

God, Death, and Evil

Soon after my return from the Aerie, I was scheduled to fulfill a previous commitment to take a ten-day visit along with several other Christians to the Shalom Hartman Institute in Jerusalem in order to study Torah and related texts with several notable rabbis. Because I had focused on the matter of anger at God, I determined, insofar as possible, to devote some of my private time in Israel to further exploring this in the form of the relationship between God and evil, generally referred to as *theodicy*. I had been particularly interested in the topic since my seminary days but never had an opportunity (or perhaps a sufficient reason) to return to it.

In brief, in traditional forms of theology, theodicy involves answering some version of the following question:

If God is both omnipotent and good, how can evil exist in God's creation?

This question quickly forces one to choose between two equally difficult alternatives: If God creates (or even allows) evil, then God is not fully good; if God cannot prevent evil, then God is not omnipotent. As far as I know, this is a conundrum that no one with a traditional theological approach has adequately settled—at least no one of whose work I am aware has offered a solution that has satisfied me.

As I thought about how my friends and family have dealt with the question, I concluded that in everyday practice, they, like most Christians, assume that God is both omnipotent and good. This assumption, however, requires them basically to ignore the theodicy question and just live with the resulting inconsistency. This is readily observable in prayers that thank and praise God for providing good things but that refrain from blaming and castigating God for bad things. The latter, blaming and castigating God for evil, would be consistent with viewing God as omnipotent, but it would also seem foolhardy at best and blasphemous at worst. It is a boundary that Christians who espouse traditional forms of theology are extremely reluctant to cross.

But cross it they do. By my observation, it has been only with the intense sense of loss that follows the death of an intimate loved one that grief pushes Christians with traditional theological viewpoints sometimes to cross the boundary. The result is anger at God: God the Omnipotent took my wife from me. Not only could God have prevented her death, God had to cause her death—that is, if God is omnipotent. And this conclusion can, in the wake of great loss, evoke anger—great anger at God. I think this may be true not only for Christians but also for those of any religious tradition that is monotheistic in character.

It was clear to me that if I looked at my situation from this standpoint, I would have reason to be angry at an omnipotent God. From such a view, it was possible to say that there was at least irony if not injustice in Veta's death. She lived her life as a devout and faithful Christian and put much of her time and energy into serving the churches she attended over the years. Furthermore, her death occurred while I was leading an effort at Claremont School of Theology to create a new model for theological education, a model intended to create a foundation for peace, harmony, and constructive collaboration among major religions. And I had the sense that I was doing so in direct response to God's urging. Unless I was totally deluded about what God was asking of me, why, in the middle of such a difficult and important undertaking, would God not only take a dedicated Christian woman but also simultaneously knock my legs out from under me by removing my chief supporter and life-mate? Even if I were deluded, would God "take" my wife just to punish me? Or forgetting about all of that, why would God take such a wonderful person anyway?

As I turned it over in my mind, I could easily feel how this prevalent view of God could cause anger—I had witnessed such anger many times. But I did not feel it. Why?

I am aware of various attempts to provide explanations of why I shouldn't be angry at God. In my view, some of these attempts exacerbate and some lessen the reason for anger, but none remove it. These explanations range from the conclusion that God is punishing the survivor (It's the result of my own sin!) to the assumption that the reason is too complex for humans to grasp and that we will understand only after we have gone to be with God. I decided that reviewing such explanations would be a good way to explore the question of theodicy.

On the plane to Israel, therefore, I reread the best recent effort to deal with theodicy I was aware of, Bart D. Ehrman, *God's Problem* (HarperCollins e-books, 2009). Though I didn't always share his conclusions, I respected Ehrman's scholarship and was aware from the first reading that the existence of evil alongside the doctrine of God's omnipotence was responsible for Ehrman's becoming agnostic, giving up his long-held belief in God in favor of professing that he just didn't know whether there is a God or not. Under the weight of Veta's death, I wanted more clearly to understand how Ehrman articulated the problem, how he analyzed it, and how he reached his conclusion as a foundation for my own reflection on it. I thought it might help me settle the theodicy question in my own mind and make a useful conclusion to my rapidly receding experience with anger.

Ehrman on Theodicy. With his careful analysis, Ehrman systematically moved through the various explanations of evil and suffering given in the Hebrew Bible and the Christian Testament. These include the views that suffering comes from God as punishment for sin; that it comes from humans as a consequence of sin; that God allows it so that God can bring good out of it, meaning that suffering is redemptive. With his characteristic directness and thoughtfulness, he dispensed with them as inadequate answers, indicating their fallacies, inconsistencies, and problems.

> Different biblical authors, as we have seen, have different explanations for all the pain and the misery: some think that pain and suffering sometimes come from God as a punishment for sin (the prophets); some think that misery is created by human beings who abuse and oppress others (the prophets again); some think that God works in suffering to achieve his redemptive purposes (the Joseph story; the Jesus story); some think that pain and misery come as

a test from God to see if his people will remain faithful to him even when it does not pay to do so (the folktale about Job); others think that we simply can't know why there is such suffering in the world—either because God the Almighty chooses not to reveal this kind of information to peons like ourselves (Job's poetry) or because it is information beyond the ken of mere mortals (Ecclesiastes). When I think about malaria, or parasites ingested through contaminated water, or other related forms of misery, pain, and death, I personally resonate much more closely with Ecclesiastes than any of the other options we've seen so far. To think that God is punishing the population of the sub-Sahara for its sins strikes me as grotesque and malevolent. They certainly aren't suffering from malaria because other human beings are oppressing them (directly), and I see nothing redemptive in their deaths, or any indication that God is merely testing them to see if they'll praise him with dying lips, wracked with pain. Maybe it is simply beyond our ability to understand. (*Problem*, 199-200)

In the end only one explanation survived his analysis and met with his approval. It was this conclusion drawn from Ecclesiastes.

Again I saw that under the sun the race is not to the swift, nor the battle to the strong, nor bread to the wise, nor riches to the intelligent, nor favor to the skillful; but time and chance happen to them all. For no one can anticipate the time of disaster. Like fish taken in a cruel net, and like birds caught in a snare, so mortals are snared at a time of calamity, when it suddenly falls upon them. (Eccles. 9:11–12)

In assessing Ecclesiastes, Ehrman wrote:

Moreover, for this author "traditional" wisdom was inherently flawed—another reason I like him so much. It simply is not true that the righteous are rewarded in life and the wicked perish: "In my vain life I have seen everything; there are righteous people who perish in their righteousness, and there are wicked people who prolong their life in their evil doing" (Eccles. 7:15); "there are righteous people who are treated according to the conduct of the wicked, and there are wicked people who are treated according to the conduct of the righteous. I said that this also is vanity" (Eccles. 8:14). The reason it is all hevel (This is the English transliteration of the Hebrew word for "vanity.") is that everyone dies and that's the end of the story: "Everything that confronts them is vanity, since the same fate comes to all, to the righteous and the wicked, to the good and the evil, to the clean and the unclean, to those who sacrifice and those who do not sacrifice. As are the good, so are the sinners … the same fate comes to everyone" (Eccles. 9:1–3). Even in this life, before death, rewards and punishments are not meted out according to merit; everything is dependent on chance. (*Problem*, 192)

Though Ehrman approved of this, it is hardly a well-rounded explanation of theodicy. It simply argues that everyone is affected by evil, albeit in unequal and unmerited ways, and that death finally ends it all for everyone. The author of Ecclesiastes refused, however, either to blame or exonerate God. Thereby the author implicitly discounts certain other explanations of theodicy found among prophetic and other writings in the Hebrew Bible. But the author of Ecclesiastes put no coherent explanation in their place, concluding only that being in such a predicament we must be content to enjoy what time we have ("eat, drink, and be merry ..." Eccles. 5:18–19).

In addition to finding the Bible unsatisfactory at trying to explain the existence of evil—God's problem—Ehrman also found other explanations lacking. The most common of these is that evil is a necessary condition for free will to exist, and God preferred that humans have free will. Indeed, this is part of the explanation offered by Process theologians. Ehrman argued simply that "free will can't solve all the problems of suffering—hurricanes in New Orleans, tsunamis in Indonesia, earthquakes in Pakistan, and so on ..." (*Problem*, 197) As a result, Ehrman was left with an insoluble quandary and a God he could not affirm. "Ultimately," he wrote, "it was the reason I lost my faith." (*Problem*, 1)

While I found Ehrman's analysis honest, thoughtful, and thorough, it did not persuade me to adopt his more traditional view of God in order to join him in angrily casting away my faith. In my view, Ehrman too quickly dismisses the Process viewpoint and works from the assumption that God is omnipotent and that God could have created a world without dangerous natural forces and other forms of "evil" without sacrificing free will. I am unconvinced on either point. As a result of his view, *God's Problem* demonstrates that Ehrman, somewhat paradoxically, continues to be exceedingly angry at the God in which he claims no longer to believe. The very tone of the book itself, as can be seen in some of the passages quoted above, demonstrates that anger clearly and repeatedly. I did not share the anger.

By the conclusion of my trip to Israel, it did not surprise me that I had not found a satisfying answer to a question that has remained a mystery for centuries. At the end of my effort, I could, however, name some competing dynamics that this particular paradox evokes. There was the option that I could blame God for my loss while simultaneously feeling as if God were sustaining me through my grief. Similarly, there was the possibility that I could hold God responsible for Veta's death while I simultaneously felt that God was weeping with me over her loss. My Process viewpoint has perspectives that relieve God of the blame and responsibility, but my childhood beginnings, steeped in a more traditional form of theology, made it possible for me to understand how coming from such a viewpoint would make it almost impossible not to blame God at least momentarily.

Once you get beyond thinking of God as an omnipotent super-person, however, it is possible to conceive that even God may have certain limits in creating and intervening in reality as we know it. But such theological speculation is neither satisfying nor conclusive. Thus, after working through the question of theodicy using Ehrman's work as a base, I reluctantly admitted that I was not likely to achieve a resolution to the paradox of the relationship of God and evil because of my limited knowledge of God and my perhaps prejudiced definition of evil.

Understanding Death—A Dream. Then it occurred to me in attempting to think through the matter of the relationship of God and evil that death doesn't necessarily always fall into the category of "evil." This, in turn, caused me to remember a dream about death that I had twenty years ago. I remembered that the dream impressed me so much that I made a written account of it. I decided to see if I could find it when I got back home.

The dream occurred at one of those times when I was facing another surgery. It was another occasion when Veta and I talked of ultimate things, preferences with regard to life support, the condition of our estate planning, how good life had been to us, and our mutual hope that I would continue to be in the picture. It was also a time when I was thinking a great deal about death, contemplating what it meant. I was by that time clearly aware that I was mortal and was past being afraid of death—I think I lost my fear of death when I went through the first surgery at the age of thirteen. Nonetheless, death is a mystery that I found to be fascinating, something I could not avoid thinking about as I made arrangements for surgery. It was then that I had the dream.

I was so eager to reread my account of the dream that I didn't unpack before digging into Veta's well-organized files. In almost no time, I found it. Here is what I had written.

> December 1990—A Dream: I have been going through a bad period. I have been blessed to have lived thirty-one years beyond all expectations but am now facing another surgery. My third prosthesis for some reason has begun to throw off blood clots. A few of them

lodged in my left eye, leaving tiny, permanent blind spots on the retina. Others caught in my spleen, causing some discomfort. Night before last, a clot reached my brain. I woke up at 4:00 a.m., got up to go to the bathroom, and fell. The entire left side of my body was "asleep," similar to when I sit too long with my legs crossed and one leg goes to sleep. I couldn't feel or use my left leg or arm.

Figuring the event was over and knowing that I was already taking anticoagulants, I managed to get back in bed and wait until morning to wake Veta and ask her to make arrangements for me to see my doctor. My episode has been diagnosed to have been a left hemispheric stroke, and my aortic prosthesis has been judged to be a ticking time bomb. Without another heart surgery (the sixth time my chest would be opened), the doctor told me that I am certain to have a stroke that will be debilitating or fatal.

With all of this weighing on my mind, I went to bed last night and had this dream:

I dreamed that I was sleeping when a messenger from God appeared before me. The messenger wore a long, brown robe with a large cowl. I could not see the messenger's face. Suddenly I became aware of the messenger addressing me with a question. It was not that I heard the question spoken aloud; rather

I perceived it directly in my mind: "What is the most brilliant and important characteristic given by God to humans?" Without pause the answer jarred me wide awake! "Death."

I got up and hobbled to the bathroom as the implications of the dream played through my mind. Humans are born to die; death is the boundary that gives meaning and urgency to life. If human life were eternal, everything would be different. We could put things off for eons and still hope to get them done—procrastination to the nth degree. Without death, we would live forever—no urgency to do anything, no urgency to accomplish anything, no urgency to love, no urgency to distinguish among values. Death is motivator, a teacher.

I know it was a dream, but I can't shake the feeling that God has sent me a message.

As I read my own account of the dream, I felt that death itself does not belong in the category of "evil." It is, rather, part of the definition of what it means to be human; it is the ultimate limit on what we call life. The circumstances surrounding how we die may (and often do) fall into the category of "evil," but the fact that death exists as the conclusion to life is not evil in and of itself.

We are prone to see death itself as evil because we don't like it; we would prefer immortality. As a part of my reading therapy, I had just read Jonathan Weiner's *Long for this World: The Strange Science of Immortality* (HarperCollins e-books: New York, 2010). Not only was the book entertaining, it reminded me of how we humans often long for, wish for, and attempt by magical and scientific means to achieve immortality. But while we have managed by means of knowledge, technology, and medicine to lengthen the average human lifespan in First World countries (I am an excellent example of that with my multiple heart surgeries and prostheses), we still have not nearly approached immortality.

As I thought all of this over, it also occurred to me that in somewhat lengthening our lives, we have not similarly improved our ability to treat one another better. By lengthening our lives, we have not made the world either a more loving or a safer place. In general, we appear to be more concerned about avoiding death than we are about the quality of the lives of those around us.

In the same folder with the account of my dream, I also found another document pertinent to the consideration of God, death, and evil. It was a note I wrote just after I had the dream. It was to be opened only in the case I did not survive the surgery, and I was not aware that Veta kept it. I had forgotten it completely. I wrote the following:

An Afterthought

December, 1990

I am leaving this afterthought because I have always felt that it is important to express what is on my heart. And my circumstance has always prompted me to express it while there was opportunity rather than later to regret not having done so. In this case, it seemed that leaving a note was most appropriate.

I don't want it to be said that my death was untimely or tragic. The event of death in and of itself is never tragic. Death is the end for which ultimate reality created us all. Tragedy lies, rather, in a life that is selfishly lived, with its potential squandered. Death is untimely only when it adds finality to a lost chance to live life usefully and fully.

As for me, by grace alone I lived many years beyond my natural time. After life itself and my family and friends, this bad heart valve may have been the greatest gift I could have received. It provided me with a fantastic range of human experience and taught me never to take a day for granted. I loved every moment of my life. I experienced the heights and depths of pleasure and pain and understood each for its uniqueness. I drank from the deep well of literature, poetry, and music. I felt the power in mountains, deserts, and wind. My work was enjoyable, constructive, and fulfilling. I knew many people and found each one to be special. I had the most wonderful child I can imagine. I met, married, and loved the woman of my dreams. I searched for my Creator. I searched, and occasionally my Creator found me. I would not change a moment of my life.

I would be flattered to know you miss my company. But don't be sad at the thought of what I might have done or what I am missing.

Think rather of how much I had. The richness
of my life—that is what is real and true. To the
end, I was amazed and thrilled by the wonder of
it all and by the alluring mystery of the Mighty
Something who created it.

If my life was not tragic, then how could my
death be tragic? No, my life was a celebration
from beginning to end. Death, for me, is the
postgame locker room of the Super Bowl victors.

I ended my deliberations on anger, God, and evil content
with the conclusion that however unexpected, unmerited, and
untimely it may have been, Veta's death did not belong in either
the category of "tragic" or "evil." God was only implicated insofar
as God created death as the necessary end for every human life.
But there was no villain, human or deity, responsible for the
timing and circumstances of her death. Anger, therefore, was
an unjustified reaction and did not merit the damage it would
do to my body and psyche if I yielded to it.

Chapter 7: Bargaining

I'll gladly take her place if you'll let me;
Make this my last request.
Take me out of this world;
God, please don't take the girl.[*]

There was hardly time to breathe between returning from Israel and leaving for the study seminar at a spiritual retreat in Wyoming known as Ring Lake Ranch. When I arranged for it (well before Veta died), I had great anticipation because it is a unique spiritual retreat center that offers a combination of serious study and outdoor activities, including my favorite: world-class fly-fishing. As I prepared to leave, however, circumstances had changed; Veta would no longer be with me (Ring Lake Ranch was one of her favorite places), and I had assigned myself the task of beginning work on the third stage of grief, *bargaining*. Since I needed time to think, and since it's a beautiful thousand miles of beautiful scenery, I decided to take my car for the journey. As preparation, I reread the brief three-and-a-half-page section on bargaining in *Grief* (17–20).

Just upon rereading the section on bargaining in *Grief*, I knew that my experience was substantially different than that described. Bargaining as described generally occurs both

---

[*] "Don't Take the Girl"; Craig M. Martin and Larry W. Johnson; recorded by Tim McGraw, 1994.

before and after the loved one dies. It occurs in advance when a loved one is ill and possibly facing death. In this circumstance, bargaining is an attempt to make a deal with God to save the loved one's life. This deal can vary from the promise to do good works or give up some bad habit to the ultimate "please, God, take my life instead of hers."

Bargaining usually recurs after the death of the loved one in one of two forms. The first form takes place in the immediate aftermath and assumes the form of begging God to "let me go to sleep, wake up, and find that this has all been a terrible dream"—all in return for some meritorious work, sacrifice, or gesture. The second form of post-death bargaining comes later and combines with guilt to generate a series of what-ifs and if-onlys. Grieving individuals typically know that these after-the-fact attempts at bargaining cannot succeed, but just the process of posing the bargain provides momentary relief from reality.

At the very outset of *Grief*, Kübler-Ross and Kessler make the point that stages notwithstanding, the grieving process is distinctive for each individual. Circumstances and life experiences act to shape and modify how each of us reacts to great loss. This was certainly true for me on the matter of bargaining.

I had virtually skipped it entirely.

Again it was the experience of open-heart surgeries that impacted my experience of the bargaining stage. As I began driving and thinking, I frankly couldn't recall whether I attempted to bargain with God that first time at age thirteen. I remembered my mother praying with me in the days leading up to the surgery and asking God to let me survive, though I could not remember her offering any bargains in the process. Her prayers were simply petitions. If she tried bargaining, I was totally unaware of it.

For the second surgery seven years later, I distinctly remembered being grateful that I had lived the "extra" seven years and being happy that a prosthesis might give me even more time. I could not remember that attempting to bargain with God ever crossed my mind.

As I reflected on this, I was profoundly shocked by the sudden resurfacing of a disturbing memory I had long buried. I remembered being embarrassed, even chagrinned, in the years between the first and second surgeries, when I somehow came into possession of a magazine devoted to Oral Roberts and faith healing. The magazine was in the format of Classic Comics and made it seem quite matter of fact that faith healing was an everyday occurrence available to all persons and applicable to all physical and spiritual maladies. The problem was that even though I had always been serious about my faith, I obviously did not have sufficient faith as a youngster to convince God to heal my heart defect before my parents were forced to resort to surgery. The magazine made my failure perfectly clear. At the time, that fact pained and worried me greatly, and just recalling it brought back those long-forgotten feelings of failure.

As I dredged up these uncomfortable memories, it occurred to me that this was the reason why I was not much into attempting to bargain with God. Since I had failed to have sufficient faith to be healed, I was clearly in no position to attempt a bargain. Why would God bargain with a person of so little faith? Sometime after that first surgery, I remember thinking that I had to forget about faith healing because the choice for a medical solution rather than a divine solution had been made. To make matters worse, the doctors advised my parents that the first surgery had only bought me a little time—a few years—but that it was not a long-term solution. I assumed, of course, that a faith healing would have been once and for all, long-term. Even though Mother continued to pray with me about my health regularly, I clearly remembered feeling that due to the circumstance, my only real option was another surgery, and I felt uncomfortable with her bringing it up because it would serve only to remind God that I was the kid with insufficient faith.

My failure of faith, therefore, gave me a heightened awareness of what I myself needed to do to recover. I might have failed to have enough faith, but I was determined that I would not fail to do everything possible on my part to make sure the surgery was successful. This determination caused me to develop a number of what are now called *biofeedback* techniques that were immensely helpful not only in enduring the surgeries but also in recuperating quickly. I had discovered biofeedback during my first surgery more or less accidentally. I found that if I prepared myself mentally, I could vastly improve the experience of otherwise traumatic events or circumstances.

Though my biofeedback activities were mostly simple, they gave me the general ability to manage pain, the capacity to reduce or eliminate the sensation of needles associated with drawing blood or getting injections, the ability to reduce my blood pressure, and the ability to remain calm and avoid anger (described above). They consisted of such things as closing my eyes and imagining that the needle about to be inserted was a "friend" and that I would feel no pain, or taking deep breaths and thinking of pleasant memories or places as the blood pressure cuff was being applied (or any other time I felt the need to relax). I would also intentionally focus on healing quickly. As a youngster, I found that doing these and other similar mental exercises materially helped improve my experience and heal faster, and I have continued them as needed to this day.

In addition to helping me recover quickly, my failure of faith was also most likely the reason that Process theology had such an appeal for me when I reached college. Whatever mechanism might be at work in faith healing—and I never assumed that it was bogus—Process suggested that it was not brought about by God's suspension of, violation of, or interruption of the laws of the universe in granting this or that petition while denying others. Rather, God is present and active in the world through the creative power of divine love, a love that does not seek outcomes through direct intervention (coercion) but through the power of persuasion.

Though at the time I didn't think of it in this way, Process provided me with an alternative to the notion that I had failed the faith test. But I do remember feeling an immense relief and excitement over Process ideas. It allowed me to see the persuasive healing power of God at work through science, technology, and medicine, giving humans the knowledge, skills, and means to accomplish miraculous things. My only failure was in holding an antiquated view of God and not understanding how miracles actually take place. I could let go of my sense of failure of faith and still, it turned out, be grateful to God for the continuation of my life.

This viewpoint moved me totally away from the idea of bargaining with God for my health. I could look for the best surgeon and hope that the doctor would be in peak form during my surgery; I could use all the physical and spiritual gifts that God makes available to me to help myself. But trying to make some kind of deal with God was pointless. According to my understanding of Process, that is not how God works.

Thus, when Veta became seriously ill, I expressed my hope through prayer that she might recover, but I did not do so by offering God a deal. I am convinced partly on the basis of my own experience that God's persuasive love can and does work miraculously through us when we align ourselves with it, so I never doubted the power of prayer. I disagreed only with some interpretations of how the power of prayer becomes effective. I did not, therefore, attempt to bargain with God during that desperate time, though I turned to God constantly to express my hope and my desperation.

As described above, after Veta died, especially during my anger, I did go through something of a what-if and if-only exercise. It was part of the process of directing blame at myself, the doctors, and the hospital and trying to assess what had gone wrong. In working through the anger stage, I was careful to articulate each of these kinds of questions and, so to speak, look each squarely in the eyes. Some of the questions were agonizing in their implications, but I thought it essential to face them.

Though I ultimately found these hypothetical questions to be irrational (if for no other reason simply because the past can't be changed) and unproductive, they continued to pop into my mind over the next few months, sparked by a comment, a sight, or my own thought process. But after focusing on them directly during the anger stage, they never carried their original intensity or their ability to be disconcerting.

When raising the what-if and if-only questions, however, I still did not find myself tempted to try to bargain with God, and neither did I try the "God, please let this all be a dream" technique. I admit having tried the latter a couple of times in the midst of particularly difficult periods during two of my early surgeries. Of course, it did not work, and it only left me feeling like an idiot for thinking it. So my own history also cured me from trying that approach.

The ruminations about bargaining kept me occupied for most of the thousand-mile trip to Ring Lake Ranch. By the time I reached Jackson Hole I had determined that I did not need to spend more time on the third stage. If it cropped up again, I would focus on it. But I was left feeling somewhat stunned by the memories of my struggle with faith healing. I had totally submerged them and had not associated them with my affinity for Process. I felt as if I had come across a new piece of information about myself that would bear further reflection.

In the meantime, I decided to take a breather from grief work and enjoy myself at Ring Lake Ranch. I needed to begin preparation for an important convocation address to take place just a month away at the opening of a new university that the school I manage and two other partner institutions had created, and Ring Lake Ranch would be an inspiring setting conducive to getting that task out of the way.

CHAPTER 8: DEPRESSION

And you don't know about sadness
Till you faced life alone;
You don't know about lonely
Till it's chiseled in stone.*

On the last leg of the journey to Ring Lake Ranch, I picked up two longtime friends. The husband of the couple was the instructor for the weeklong session I had chosen to attend. As a couple, Veta and I had known them for twenty-five years. When we arrived at the ranch, I knew there would be another set of longtime friends whom Veta and I had known for forty-two years—almost all of the years we had been married. This, combined with the experience of arriving back at a place that I had never visited without Veta at my side, and moving into the same cabin we had shared on previous occasions, had an immediate and powerful effect on me.

It was not the same effect as the earlier disbelief I had experienced at home; it was more like a distancing from the reality around me. Before long everyone knew of my loss and to a person were supportive and affirming. I, in turn, tried to be cordial and grateful, but I was having an almost out-of-body experience. I felt as if I were standing aside and watching myself

---

* "Chiseled in Stone"; Max D. Barnes and Vern Gosden; recorded by Vern Gosden, 1989.

go through the social motions. I was especially self-conscious during mealtimes, the principal times when the whole group would get together. We would laugh, talk, exchange accounts of how our days were going, and generally catch up with existing acquaintances and make new friends. But I felt like my part of conversations was artificial; I felt like I was acting—as if in a play. And all the while, I felt as if I were also watching the play.

This was, I believe, how *depression* set in with me. I felt outside of the loop, like an extra thumb. Everywhere there were couples; I had previously been part of a couple. I was self-conscious and didn't feel that I fit in anymore. In retrospect, I have some idea of the dynamics that drove such feelings. In my new status as a widower, I was no longer a fit with the group, not because anyone wanted to keep me out, but because as a single I didn't know how to fit back in and they didn't know how to fit me back in. When I was part of a couple, how others perceived me was at least partially filtered through their perception of Veta. I certainly felt different without her, and perhaps they did not know how (or what) to think of me without her.

Fortunately, our frequent fly-fishing excursions provided me with some relief. It was easier to feel things were more normal during the times I went fly-fishing with my two buddies. None of our wives were the least bit interested in fly-fishing, so it was a setting where Veta's absence did not leave me feeling strange. This temporary relief, however, could not offset the emotional impact of the whole experience.

To make matters worse, the program my friend was offering was on the Southern woman writer Flannery O'Connor. Given my state of mind, a more dismal, depressing writer could not have been chosen. While I have over the years enjoyed O'Connor's work, I was hard-pressed to read and discuss O'Connor's dark fiction, rife with murder and a host of other tragic elements, given my state of mind. It was for me personally an unfortunate topic to take on at the point where I was in the grief process. It added emotional fuel to the as yet unrecognized embers of depression.

I had set myself the task of beginning work on the opening convocation address to be given in early September. I actually enjoy writing and giving such addresses, so my third evening at Ring Lake Ranch, I sat down with my computer to begin writing. The ideas and words wouldn't come. It was as if my mind couldn't focus. I was surprised and irritated. I sat in an unproductive fog for more than an hour and had nothing to show. I had not a single useful idea about where to focus the address. I had not written a word.

This was the moment when it dawned on me that, in deference to my grief calendar, depression had not waited for me to return from Wyoming. I was experiencing symptoms of depression. With this realization, I pulled out *Grief* and confirmed it. My feelings of being outside the loop, of going through the motions, of being unable to be productive were there. Putting aside my effort to get a start on my convocation address, I decided I needed to spend some time thinking about myself and depression and determining how I could deal with it in the most constructive way.

For many reasons, I did not like the idea of being overcome by any emotion, especially depression. Because of what its long-term effects could be if it moved into clinical depression, it was the stage that I feared most. Moreover, in a practical vein, it was already August 3, and I had slightly over one month to write an address that would be important in the evolution of the organization for which I was responsible. This was precisely why I had taken a straightforward approach to dealing with my need to grieve. It was clear to me that if any stage of grief could disrupt my attempt to structure and manage grief, it would be depression. If I could not find a constructive way forward, I would fail in my effort to manage grief and also let a lot of people down.

That evening I set myself the task of finding a way through depression that would leave room for me to function. Feeling some urgency, I wanted to break through depression by the time I returned (August 22, 2010) from the last of my summer travels, to Chautauqua, New York. That would give me two weeks to break through depression, enough to be able to write the address. The way I was feeling, that goal seemed unrealistic, actually more like a joke.

Early the next morning, looking out at the lake from cabin 8A, I saw an osprey catch a good-sized trout and carry it back to its nest. Birds of prey have always been signs of hope for me, and just the sight of it was encouraging. I had long ago discovered the mind-body-spirit relationship and benefitted from that discovery. There was no rational reason why the sight of an osprey should fill me with encouragement, but that is what I had come to expect at the sight of a bird of prey. There is also no rational reason that it should appear just when I needed it most, but it did. The effect was positive and palpable. Just as surely as I had been able to manage pain, I was at that moment convinced that there had to be a way to mediate the impact of depression. I just needed to create some kind of biofeedback process adapted for depression. I decided to start by taking a hard, unflinching look at what I was feeling and how that added up to depression.

I was not concerned whether my analysis of depression would be medically correct. It only needed to help me understand my own situation and give me a way to move forward. As I thought about it, I couldn't find a single, identifiable focus for depression. Unlike the other stages, it didn't have a unique character. Then it occurred to me that perhaps depression was related to all that had come before. While I had gotten through the stages of disbelief (denial), anger, and all of the thoughts triggered by the business of bargaining, each of them had left an emotional residue. I remembered a soap commercial that accused other soaps of leaving "an unseen sticky film." It was as if an unseen sticky residue from the previous stages of grief had built up, and the cumulative effect was so heavy that depression was the result.

I thought about why the idea of being depressed made me uneasy. During my Duke years, I had gotten to know William Styron. He was a friend of the library and had donated his literary archives to the university. In order to support the library, Styron would occasionally give a private lecture to Friends of the Library gatherings in New York. On one such occasion, he had talked candidly about the circumstances that led to his writing *Darkness Visible: A Memoir of Madness*, a book that chronicled his serious bout with depression. I knew from that lecture, from the book, and from my personal conversations with him that serious depression could be debilitating and was not in any way to be taken lightly. I remembered Styron's gripping and frightening description of his depression and knew that I had to avoid slipping into the kind of depression he suffered if at all possible.

It was reasonable to assume that the depression I was feeling was not of the deep, clinical kind that afflicted Styron—an illness, he concluded, likely stemming from the death of his mother when he was a child of nine and exacerbated by a number of other factors over the course of his life. While what I was feeling was grief-related and situational, it had not festered emotionally unresolved for years, and I hoped that it would not become more complex or prove to be long-lasting.

By the end of the day, I had decided that I would make an effort by myself to confront my depression in order to keep it from worsening. I could only hope that I would not get to the point of needing to seek counseling. I hastily worked out a three-step approach to coping with the depression that was settling over me. Though simple, the steps were the best that I could come up with in the moment. The steps included the following:

1. initiating a process of desensitizing myself to the residue of the preceding stages;
2. developing a competing set of positive perspectives, expectations, and activities that would emphasize the vitality of ongoing life; and
3. continually reminding myself that depression was only a stage that I would pass through.

This third step, I decided, should begin immediately and become something regular, something I would use like a mantra to remind myself that my grief, including depression, was temporary and on a calendar. It would run like a refrain through the efforts involved in steps one and two.

Confronting Depression

Denial and Disbelief Revisited. Forty years earlier, when I was in my first library job, the US was still in the midst of the sexual revolution that began in the 1960s. I was taken aback when a faculty member came to me and asked if I would acquire for the library some graphically explicit but not "kinky" pornographic films. Surprised at the request, I asked why he wanted me to do such a thing. The reason, he indicated, was that he had been asked to teach a new course on human sexuality for the seminary. It seemed, he said, that in the past ministers lacked the grounding to deal with sexual issues with equanimity and wisdom, partly because it was a taboo subject excluded from their education. The faculty member told me that he intended to require students to say out loud in class a list of taboo words and then view and discuss the films. The pornographic films and the taboo words were part of an educational regimen intended to desensitize students to the shock of the common human practice of sexuality and the language (both formal and slang) associated with it so that they could get past embarrassment and learn how to understand and deal with the sexual dysfunction being experienced by those for whom they would eventually provide counsel. This kind of desensitizing was, he thought, necessary if they were to be able to get over their own repression, embarrassment, and difficulties in order to serve those who sought help from them with regard to issues of human sexuality.

I never knew if that particular effort to desensitize students was effective; I only remember the fact that it took place, and I knew that I needed a way to deal with my current situation. So I decided that I would use a similar approach in my own desensitizing from the emotional residue of the first three stages. I determined that I would do so by explicitly attempting to recall and sort through my feelings during the first stages of grief, a task that should not be difficult since they were so fresh.

Fearing that this would not be enough, I also decided to make a special effort to listen to a number of agonizingly sad country songs. I would force myself to listen to them over and over—basically overdose myself on the most maudlin, heart-wrenching, pitiful lyrics I could find. And I knew there were some seriously tear-your-heart-out-sad songs.

Thanks to iTunes technology, I had my music collection on my laptop, so I began that evening to put together a grief playlist of twenty songs (see below) that would accomplish the purpose. Of course, the exact circumstances of the songs would not necessarily be a perfect match for my circumstance, but that didn't matter as long as they were evocative of similar pain. It was the bathos I needed—to be plunged into the common human experience of the pain of loss.

As the playlist began to take shape, one of the first songs I added was Kris Kristofferson's "Loving Her Was Easier." Not only are the lyrics evocative, it was a song that Veta and I had listened to and enjoyed together particularly during the early years of our marriage. It was still on our "favorites" nostalgia list, and it put me emotionally squarely back in the midst of our loving relationship. The stage could not have been better set for recalling the earlier stages of my grief.

It was midweek when I began to work on recalling and re-experiencing the first of those first three stages (denial and disbelief). Without intending it, I found myself matching some of the songs on my list to the denial stage. As a result, I combined working on the first stage with listening repeatedly to two songs in particular. The lyrics of Hugh Prestwood's song "Ghost in this House" sum up precisely how the first stage hit me: When Veta died, I felt like a ghost in my own house. And the melancholy voice of Vern Gosden singing "Chiseled in Stone" was grippingly true to my feelings of being alone with the abject finality of the death of the one I loved. Beginning with recalling my first experience of disbelief, the memory and the music immediately plunged me into deep angst and self-pity. Memory and music together—raw grief, sad lyrics, and mournful music—constituted a powerful emotional trigger for me.

Late into the Wyoming evenings for the rest of that week, with the help of earbuds so as not to disturb my next-door neighbors, I recalled the disbelief I experienced. I tried hard to remember specifics related to beginning with the experience of the empty houses in which it seemed like Veta would walk out of the next room at any moment. I closed my eyes and imagined standing in my Upland and North Carolina houses. I thought of the colors of the walls, the way furnishings were arranged in the rooms, and the furniture we had chosen together. I let myself feel it all over again, sitting there in the cabin where Veta and I had been together on our last visit to Ring Lake Ranch.

As I passed the rest of the week, I also thought about the tasks that now fell to me. These included the many tasks that I had struggled to fit into my schedule and the numerous important things especially relating to my vanishing social contacts that were no longer done. I knew that these elements of workload and isolation affected me deeply and were conducive to feeling some amount of depression. I realized that part of my growing depression had to do with the long-term priority I had for using otherwise idle home time as additional work time. I remember once reading a study that found that highly productive people often got more done than their peers simply because they worked longer hours. I knew that I had fit that category for many years, but that now it was a category that would simply no longer work for me. I decided I would consciously change my priorities so that I didn't experience guilt for not bringing work home. Instead, I would place a higher value on taking care of the various details of my personal life. I would do so because the reality of my situation was not going to change.

As the end of the week approached and my return drive to

California loomed, I thought I should shift to revisit the second stage anger during the return road trip. Before doing so on my last night at Ring Lake Ranch, I deliberately sat and reviewed the matter of denial and disbelief once again. I recalled my first attempt to put my own stamp on the bedroom by turning a small desk that had been only ornamental into a functioning desk. It stood in a dark corner and required a lamp in order for me to see to work at the desk. So I went to a lighting equipment store and spent time looking at all the lamps. I looked for the one that appealed to *my* taste this time rather than *our* taste. I found one that suited me, purchased it, took it home, assembled it, and put it on the desk. Less than twenty-four hours later I was downstairs in a room that housed our piano where, for the first time, I actually noticed the last lamp that Veta had purchased. It was exactly the same lamp I had just purchased for the desk in the bedroom.

At the time my experience with the lamp occurred, I laughed, thinking how similar our tastes had been. There at Ring Lake Ranch, however, I had the additional insight that, in fact, Veta's taste had rubbed off on me. I could not claim to have any conscious sense of taste, matching styles, or color schemes before knowing Veta. I was able that night to conclude that in a way Veta was still present in the effect she had on me. I decided I would no longer think of her as absent so much as present with me in a different way. I would consciously attempt to enjoy the vestiges of her presence that remained in the manner in which she had furnished and decorated our houses and the ways she had become a part of me.

Revisiting denial, therefore, had given me something new and positive, a way to start thinking about Veta beyond the mere fact of having lost her. I hoped it would help me begin to shake the grip of depression, and I reminded myself that this could be a pleasant experience. As promised, I also reminded myself that depression was a passing stage.

More importantly, reviewing my experience of the first stage of grief convinced me of something I had not previously grasped, namely, that *the grief process is not only the way that we humans deal with the loss of those we love; it could also become the vehicle for personal growth.* By this I mean that even there in the midst of the stage labeled *depression*, I had the distinct feeling that I was learning and growing personally and spiritually as a result of struggling with the loss of Veta. When this thought hit me, I wanted to reject it on an emotional level. How could that be? How could the death of the person I loved, my best friend and closest confidant, become the catalyst for my personal growth? I hated the idea. But my mind would not let it go; if I could survive the loss, I would somehow become stronger, wiser, and (perhaps) a better human being. That night, against my wishes, this thought bounced repeatedly through my mind like an echo: *use grief not only to deal with my loss but also as the means to become a better person.*

My Grief List of Sad Country Songs

- "A Good Year for the Roses"
- "A Picture of Me without You"
- "A Place to Fall Apart"
- "Chiseled in Stone"
- "Cold Hard Truth"
- "Don't Take the Girl"
- "Ghost in This House"
- "Go Rest High on That Mountain"
- "Got No Reason Now for Going Home"
- "He Stopped Loving Her Today"

- "How She Could Sing the Wildwood Flower"
- "It's Not Easy; Ribbon of Darkness"
- "Learning to Live Again"
- "Look at Us"
- "Loving Her Was Easier"
- "Never Knew Lonely"
- "(She's Just) An Old Love Turned Memory"
- "The Beaches of Cheyenne"
- "The Dance; Only the Lonely"
- "When My Blue Moon Turns to Gold"

Back to Anger. Saturday morning, I said goodbye to friends old and new at Ring Lake Ranch and began the long drive back to Southern California. I was ready to revisit anger, only now in light of the persistent idea that I should stay alert to opportunities for personal and spiritual growth.

But first I plugged my iPod with the list of sad songs into the *aux* port in the dash of my car and turned on the radio.

It took me the first two hundred miles or so to get "cried out." I wallowed in the heartbreaking misery represented in the lyrics and used almost a full box of tissues. And then the sad songs began to lose their effect; for some reason that I don't understand, the desensitizing worked. The urge to cry finally lost its grip on me. Though I did break into tears a few times after my return trip, my weeping was never again so frequent or intense.

As my weeping slowed, I turned my thoughts to the stage of anger.

I recalled the anger I had felt and the times I had set aside to "let it run." The most intense anger had been self-directed, with anger at the doctors and hospital being next in intensity.

In endeavoring to review it, I found no residual; the anger was gone.

But there was something else that had eluded my consciousness when I went through anger on my grief calendar. It was a kind of aftermath that followed anger. As I experienced it, my anger turned out to be futile, at least in terms of useful results. Anger may have given me a way to express my pain, but mentally jabbing at myself, the doctors, and the hospital accomplished nothing. That is one of the defects of anger as I experienced it; it resulted in no tangible, positive outcome.

It was my conclusion to the stage of anger that there was no one to blame for Veta's death and, by implication, that anger was inappropriate. I still found anger to be an accurate characterization of how I had felt, but beyond that I discovered a feeling of dejection. When there is nothing and no one to blame—even one's self—there is no resolution. While there was no residue of anger, there was another residue—a residue of futility.

Summing up Depression

After a long day of driving and reviewing my experience of anger, I stopped for the night near the town of St. George, Utah. As I reflected on the day, it was suddenly easy for me to see how depression was a legitimate successor to anger. The dejection and futility I was feeling were roommates with depression. Indeed, it then occurred to me that the same was true for each of the first three stages. Though I had found a positive perspective on denial and disbelief, it was nonetheless true that with regard to the main issue, Veta was not coming back. No matter how I dealt with stage one, the ending was the same; she was gone, not to return. The resulting emptiness was conducive to depression. Similarly, the outcome of stage three bargaining in the grief process is necessarily failure. One cannot bargain the dead back to life. I remembered verses from Thomas Gray's "Elegy Written In A Country Churchyard" that I had committed to memory years earlier:

Can storied urn or animated bust
Back to its mansion call the fleeting breath?
Can Honour's voice provoke the silent dust,
Or Flattery soothe the dull cold ear of Death?

Nothing reverses the reality of death—not even bargaining with God. Even though I did not engage in bargaining, the very process of reflecting on its futility added to my feeling of emptiness.

Thus in my own thinking I concluded that, indeed, the fourth stage, depression, was the unavoidable accumulation of the futility resident in the first three stages. Even my losing the urge to cry with the sad, sad country music represented a kind of futility and emptiness. Crying does nothing to change reality. The appearance of depression for me occurred, therefore, as I finally and fully understood intellectually and emotionally that Veta was gone and I was alone. If there was anything positive to say about depression, it was that it represented the moment that I gave up the futile efforts represented in the first three stages to fight the reality of Veta's death.

Now the challenge was to keep this moment of giving up those futile efforts from escalating into the kind of serious depression that could destroy my ability to function effectively or, worse, result in my own death. Sitting in that motel, I could clearly feel the kind of negative progression that occurred through the stages and that could result in the broken heart syndrome.

I pondered my conclusion with regard to depression the next day on the last leg of my return home. What I had on the positive side was a way to remember and appreciate Veta and the environments she created in our houses. It was the first time I was able to think of her without the crushing pain of losing her forcing itself into my thoughts. More importantly, I had the continuing feeling that grief could be the catalyst for personal growth.

On the not-so-positive side, I was certain that I had entered stage four depression, but at least I felt as if I knew how it was a natural outgrowth of the three previous stages.

Chautauqua

On the heels of my return from Wyoming, I traveled to Chautauqua, New York, for a week to attend a series of programs related to my work. Even though I had gained some perspective on my depression on the trip to Wyoming, I had not shaken the depression; I still felt as though I was just going through the motions. The week at Chautauqua was filled with excellent programs and the opportunity to meet several extraordinary thought and spiritual leaders, but programs and personalities didn't brighten my spirits.

On the next to the last day before I left Chautauqua, however, I attended a program that proved to be the key to breaking through the depression. The program was an exercise consisting of a meditation based on the seven-stage Buddhist Metta practice of compassion. The meditation was led by a distinguished Buddhist monk and was profoundly effective in focusing my entire attention on compassion. The effect of the meditation when it is regularly practiced is to help the practitioner gradually become more compassionate in every thought and action. It is a means of conditioning oneself to align thoughts and actions.

That night as I lay in bed thinking of the experience, it occurred to me that perhaps I could use the seven-stage meditation as a means to help myself deal with the residue of regret, loneliness, and guilt that I felt were behind my depression. I had still found no comfort in the pattern of prayer typical of my Protestant upbringing, so this seemed like a constructive alternative. I got out of bed and wrote the following meditation.

A Meditation after the Death of a Loved One
I will think of Veta every day.
I will grieve her death in a positive way.
I will not let my grief shorten my life.
I will forgive myself for not being able to save her.
I will become a stronger and better person
for having the years with her.
I will celebrate and be joyful for the beauty she
brought and the good works she did.
I will perpetuate her compassionate ways.

I found it difficult to articulate each line, but the fourth line was especially difficult. My struggle demonstrated to me that even after attempting to deal with the feeling of guilt and self-anger, they were still with me. After writing the meditation, I spent the next half-hour putting it into practice according to the manner demonstrated earlier that afternoon in the guided meditation on compassion.

When I had concluded the meditation, I was surprised to find that I was experiencing a feeling of relief. For the first time since Veta's death, I was also aware that I was feeling a glimmer of hope. These feelings were enough to cause me to decide that I would employ the meditation each day upon awaking in the morning and before going to sleep at night.

As I went back to bed, I had a new confidence that I could break through the depression in time to write the address for the rapidly approaching convocation.

Back at home and at work with only a few days left, I sat down at my desk again to attempt to draft the convocation address, and this time the words came. At the end of the day, with a draft in hand, I knew that I was not finished with depression, but I was confident that it would not keep me from being able to carry out my responsibilities. I also felt some ironic relief that the fall, if it were in any way typical, would overwhelm me with a workload that would not let up until Thanksgiving. Perhaps the distraction of work would lessen the impact of depression and help me move on to the fifth and final stage of my grief calendar.

A Positive Agenda

I had also decided that laying out a positive agenda—one that would give me something of a renewed zest for life— could help counteract depression. Finding such an agenda for one in my state of mind, however, proved to be difficult, and I could not immediately think of anything to get started. It was precisely then that a couple, Gene and Charky, two of my dearest friends, rescued me with an unexpected proposal. They were spending a period of time in Australia early that fall and were returning in October with a connection through New Zealand. If I could manage to get to New Zealand near the time of their connecting flight, she would fly home, and he would remain in New Zealand to join me for a fly-fishing expedition to the South Island. It was just what I needed, something different, compelling, and challenging to kick-start the effort to develop a positive agenda. I leapt at the opportunity.

As it turned out, the timing of the proposed fishing expedition worked perfectly in conjunction with a business trip I was taking to South Korea. I could fly to New Zealand, fly-fish with Gene, then continue on to South Korea. It occurred to me that since I would have my fishing gear, I could also explore the possibility of fly-fishing in South Korea on one of the days that was not booked for work. Both possibilities came to fruition and did, I believe, help me make progress toward shaking free from depression.

Fly-fishing on New Zealand's South Island proved to be an extraordinary experience. We stayed in a lodge that had been hand-built by the couple that ran it. It was a 6,000-square-foot marvel that had its own home-generated sources of electricity and water. It was a model of economy and sustainability. The owners used only the most energy-efficient lights and appliances and operated for a fraction of the cost of much smaller houses in most other parts of the world. It was interesting, instructive, and inspiring for one who had grown up accustomed to the Western, energy-wasteful style.

The owners were also gourmet cooks—no ordinary fishing camp fare was served. Each meal was exotic and exceptionally good; I might have gone just for the cuisine had I known what would be in store. And the owners were delightful, friendly, and full of information about New Zealand.

It would have been sufficient for me just to enjoy our hosts, experience their lodge and food, and see the country. The South Island is where the filming took place for the film version of J. R. R. Tolkien's *Lord of the Rings*. The north end of the South

Island, our destination, offers a rugged and startlingly beautiful setting, almost unbelievable in its character—which, of course, is why it was chosen as the setting for the film. It provided a real-world setting that matched the magnificent, mythical world described in the book. Just being there and experiencing the grandeur from the view from the lodge was astounding.

Equally astounding was the fly-fishing. The fish we sought were brown trout. Like other species of trout, the brown trout were introduced to New Zealand in the late 1860s from Europe. There in the pure, crystal-clear rivers, the brown trout grow to prodigious size—so large are they that the style of fly-fishing is sight-driven: spot and stalk. That is, you don't simply cast randomly, hoping to catch one of the huge fish. Instead, the process is to move carefully upstream looking for a large, usually solitary trout and then to cast to the specific fish that has been spotted. If the casting is done poorly, the large trout—that is also wild and wary—will disappear.

We had five great days of fishing, often in beautiful, remote locations. Twice we traveled to and from our fishing destination by helicopter, flying over the astoundingly rugged and beautiful scenery. Our local fishing guide was a master, and with his knowledge of entomology and the rivers, both of us caught plenty of big trout. At one of the locations on the Crowe River that we reached by helicopter, I was fortunate enough to catch a fish that at the time was the largest on record to have been taken from the Crowe.

It was, in short, a storybook fishing trip, and in spite of my depression, I enjoyed the company of my old friend Gene, the fishing, and myself. On the long flight from Auckland to Seoul, I felt a glimmer of optimism. And I reminded myself that once again, without a maudlin word, two dear friends, Gene and

Charky, had found the perfect way to begin to renew my zest for life.

To put the icing on the cake, the working part of the trip to South Korea also went well. My colleagues and I worked a hard, non-stop schedule during which we enjoyed existing friends and made new friends. We ended our obligations with some time left, and one of my colleagues had mentioned my interest in fly-fishing to one of our South Korean hosts. As a result, I was given the unexpected opportunity to fish for one of the two trout species in South Korea, the Lennox (Mongolian trout), guided by perhaps the best known fly-fishing expert in South Korea. While only one day, this too was an extraordinary expedition in the streams and mountains on the West coast of South Korea. In addition to catching (and releasing) a Lennox, I came away with new friends and a memorable experience.

Though it happened largely because my colleague arranged it, this trip that combined fly-fishing and work, especially following the exhilarating New Zealand outing, reassured me that my experience of depression was resolving and would not deepen. On the long plane ride home, I reflected on the fact that while fly-fishing I had felt the old familiar appreciation that had always characterized my time in the natural world, enhanced by the company of a longtime friend, and I was convinced that I could again enjoy life. I was also aware that in relating to our South Korean constituencies, I had also enjoyed my role as president; I was carrying out my role in more than a perfunctory manner.

I felt as if the grip of depression was broken. While I might experience the remnants of its effects, I felt as if it would not be for me a debilitating, long-term disability.

CHAPTER 9: ACCEPTANCE

I'm gonna smile my best smile,
And I'm gonna laugh like it's going out of style,
Look into her eyes and pray that she don't see
That learning to live again is killing me.*

I had roughly scheduled November to be the beginning of the fifth and last stage of grief, *acceptance*. By the time I arrived home from Korea, I felt that I was functioning sufficiently well that I could begin to move out of depression and explore life without Veta. As was my custom, I started by reviewing once again the previous stages. In doing so, I focused especially on the fourth and most frightening stage, depression. I wanted to be certain that I had, indeed, gotten through it sufficiently to try acceptance.

Though I didn't actually know how to measure my progress in overcoming depression, I decided simply to trust my feelings. And my feelings told me that I was no longer in that paralyzed state of suspension that I had experienced in Wyoming. I concluded, therefore, that I should monitor my feelings and move forward.

November 5–7, 2010, Baton Rouge—Field Testing the "New Normal". One of the first tests of my readiness to move forward

---

* "Learning to Live Again"; Don Schlitz and Stephanie Davis; recorded by Garth Brooks, 1993.

came in early November. I'm on the Board of Experts of an institute located at Louisiana State University (LSU), and each fall the Board meets on the LSU campus. The institute was established by two more wonderful friends whose company Veta and I had enjoyed together. The fall meeting is timed to coincide with one of the major football games of the year and concludes with attending the big game. I knew that going to the board meeting would give me a good idea of my progress because Veta had accompanied me on each of my previous trips, and going alone would present me with the full emotional gamut.

The trip lived up to my expectations. Traveling the same route alone reminded me at every turn of what it was like with Veta by my side: Entering the room in the hotel where I had never been without her reminded me; dining in the hotel restaurant reminded me. At the board meeting, my board colleagues expressed their condolences. And the dinner with our friends took place in a restaurant where I had never been without Veta's company. Yet, while I was acutely aware of Veta's absence, I was not undone by any of the venues. More importantly, I was beginning to feel accustomed to my new solitary presence.

I knew that I was experiencing what for me would be (in a somewhat overused phrase) the new normal, and I was beginning to feel as if it would be okay. On the other hand, it didn't yet seem totally real. Even though I was feeling more comfortable, there was still an uncertainty lingering around the edges.

It would take a dramatic event to remove my uncertainty with clarity and finality.

A Startling Final Metaphor. As Thanksgiving approached, I decided to repeat an old custom and spend Thanksgiving with my brother and his wife at their home in Northwest Texas. In my younger years, all the males of the family returned for the Thanksgiving holidays to the Campbell Ranch. It was a time of male bonding centered primarily around hunting. Though we had not observed the custom recently, my brother's home is an easy drive from the ranch, so I made plans to travel to Texas in order to spend some time with him and my sister-in-law and visit the ranch again.

The plan came together as I had hoped, and on Thanksgiving, my brother and I traveled to the ranch. That particular year, I had decided to hunt with a camera rather than a gun, and the hunting was good. It was also wonderful and emotionally healing to have the time with my brother.

On the Friday following Thanksgiving (November 26, 2010), Black Friday, as it is commonly known, the West Texas wind was unusually calm, so we decided it was safe to use the outdoor grill to prepare lunch. As it happened, a spark flew from the grill and set fire to the dry grass. The home water well had gone dry from a persistent drought, so we had no water with which to fight the fire. In moments it had spread in every direction, setting fire to a hundred-year-old bunkhouse that stood adjacent to the ranch house. The flames from the bunkhouse shot many feet into the air and set fire to the house.

Seeing immediately that the fire was well beyond the ability of my brother and me to control, we called the local volunteer fire department. In the end, it took the fire departments from six of the small regional towns working together for two and a half hours to put out the fire. They had concentrated on controlling its progress through the grass and brush, lest a conflagration destroy the entire countryside. As it was, the fire report indicated that approximately 150 acres had been burned, along with a house.

The ranch house was totally destroyed. At some point during the two-and-a-half-hour drama, I looked at the house being consumed with fire, heard the rifle cartridges stored there exploding, thought of the computer and grief calendar I had left there with my notes about grieving, and had a profound personal epiphany: the house and everything in it were gone and could not be recovered; and Veta, like the house I saw going up in smoke, was just as gone. That stark, absolute reality struck me like one of the exploding cartridges in that moment of stifling smoke and flames. The house suddenly became for me a metaphor for the loss of Veta. She, like the house and all that was in it, was irretrievably gone and unrecoverable. She would never return.

On the drive back to my brother's home, with a certain emotional fatigue, I knew that looking back was fruitless. The only useful option was to look forward. The past is for remembering, the future for living.

That evening, the conversation between my brother, his wife, and myself started with an understandably somber tone, reflecting on the loss. But it quickly took a positive turn; I wanted—I *needed*—to build a new house. So did they. We began to brainstorm how we could do so. Before the evening ended, we had even sketched out a floor plan for the new place. By the time we went to bed, it's fair to say that there was at least a little excitement in the air.

As I lay in bed that night, I found myself feeling that I could also rebuild my life. It was the first time since Veta's death that I found myself thinking about the future in terms of possibilities rather than in terms of dealing with pain and loss.

Closing a Lid On the Past. For the Christmas holidays, I returned to my home in North Carolina. I was accompanied for the first part of my stay by the same friend George who, with his wife Linda, had been with me for my return there during the previous summer. We had a great time that Christmas preparing wonderful meals, watching it snow, and generally enjoying one another's company.

When George departed, I spent time reflecting on how important those friends, along with other friends and family, had been in helping me get through my grief. It was not, I thought, anything that they or others said that helped sustain me; it was simply that they had been with me at critical moments. Their unsolicited acts of kindness also helped me when I was most in need of help. Those acts included gathering Veta's clothes, helping me give the clothes away, involving me in activities, and simply staying in touch.

When such loss happened to my friends, I now knew that I couldn't comfort them with words, I would just be present for them as they worked through their grief. It isn't that words cannot be helpful, but no words are sufficient to ameliorate the feeling of loss or replace the grief work one must go through identified by the stages. When I was in the midst of grief, nothing anyone said could suddenly short-circuit the emotional pain. I simply had to deal with my feelings of pain, face the fact of loss, and gradually move on with life.

On January 2, 2011, I had an airline ticket to return home to California. My route home required me to drive south from North Carolina to Atlanta, Georgia, and then to fly across country. During both the driving and flying, I thought back through the stages of grief I had experienced during the nine-and-a-half months since Veta's death. It felt to me as if my grief had been something like a bell curve, with the stage of depression being the height of my malaise. After that, beginning with the trip to New Zealand and culminating with the burning of the ranch house, I had begun to set my mind on the future.

By the time I arrived back in my California home, I felt with growing confidence that the choice to move forward with life, a choice I had made in the midst of disbelief and agony only days after Veta's death, was the right choice. I could, I thought, continue to live with purpose and pursue a fulfilling life. In doing so, I would endeavor to remember the past with appreciation and pleasure but live for the future.

I needed, I thought, something like a ceremonial act to mark this moment; it would be yet another point in my life when I would mark a new beginning. Though I had not planned it, that ceremonial act happened when I took off the wedding band that Veta had put on my finger forty-four years earlier, placed it in my jewelry box, and closed the lid. When the lid snapped shut, I was suddenly taken by the awareness that a major era in my life had closed along with that box lid.

CHAPTER 10: FINAL REFLECTIONS

'Cause from here to the end is what matters, my friend,
And you're right at the peak of your form,
Still in the eye of the storm.*

Important Lessons

From Loneliness to Solitude. Being alone and its frequent corollary loneliness have been common to the human experience for ages, and whether by chance or by choice, it is the situation that defines the private time of many in this and other cultures today. Nonetheless, because I had always enjoyed healthy relationships with family and friends, I had never focused on the implications and challenges of being alone.

When my circumstances changed, I remembered that one of my college professors, Dr. Howard Slatte, once said that an educated person is someone who can be by him- or herself and still not be alone. His point was that if you read books, listen to music, or appreciate art, you can remain present and engaged with others by means of the life of your mind. I had always remembered that idea but never really had an opportunity to understand its value. But after Veta died, I suddenly had

---

* "Eye of the Storm"; Kris Kristofferson; recorded by Kris Kristofferson and Willie Nelson, 1984.

occasion to think about how I would fill the void created by her absence.

At first, of course, coming home to an empty house I turned on the television. It was a most dissatisfying experience. Not having watched much television in my recent adult life, I found the programming to be largely vacuous, superficial, and quite inadequate and unhelpful for one in my circumstance. To me, it was merely a shallow distraction that prevented me from thinking or getting anything practical done. I remember turning it off with the amusing thought that I could now probably tolerate salespersons who make uninvited phone calls—at least they are someone to talk with.

As I experimented with filling my time alone at home, I found music and reading (reading unrelated to my work) to be considerably more satisfying than television. Both reading and listening to music are good, soul-soothing therapy. I find them to be directly beneficial to my grieving and also intellectually stimulating. I came to feel that they provided me with both intellectual and spiritual nourishment, and I have made them a continuing part of my routine.

I also began to enjoy the time I set aside just to think. I had long made thinking a discipline related to my work, but now I made a list of topics not related to work that I wanted to explore and divided my thinking time into two parts: research and investigation, and deliberation and thinking. Initially I focused the topics on my situation and the stages of grief. Ultimately, I found such deliberate thinking to be so enjoyable and beneficial that I branched out with my selection of subjects. There are topics that defy definitive resolution (like *theodicy*—the problem of the relationship of God and evil) and others that have more satisfying resolution. I liked working on some of each type. I found this kind of deliberate thinking to be so useful that I have also made it an ongoing part of my routine.

Similarly, engaging in spiritual practices was another area that I came more fully to explore as a result of being alone. Though I had for many years engaged in spiritual practices, I had focused on some more than others and never had time to explore a group of them simultaneously to the degree I wished. So it was that I set out to satisfy my interest in spiritual practices. I returned to an older book that continues to be reprinted as a format for my effort (Richard J. Foster, *Celebration of Discipline: The Path to Spiritual Growth*, 1988). For me, it was a good place to start, and I believe that engaging in spiritual practices helped me live through my grief by strengthening me not only spiritually but also emotionally. As a result, I have made spiritual practices a continuing part of my life.

The result is that being alone for extended periods of time no longer leaves me feeling lonesome. Though being alone was thrust upon me in a painful and sudden way, I have come to appreciate its value. Solitude does not ultimately remove my desire for a degree of human contact and relationship, but I can understand and appreciate its appeal to those who choose to pursue an ascetic way of life. I didn't find the degree of isolation characteristic of an entirely ascetic lifestyle to be a suitable personal goal, but I have made time for much more silence and solitude in my daily routine.

The Five Stages of Loss. It can be argued that attempting to identify five stages of loss that are common to the human experience after the death of a loved one is misguided. After all, we are all different, with considerable variations in our response to many things. Because I am neither a psychologist nor a pastoral counselor, there is a certain level of this argument that I am not qualified to join. I am, however, qualified to reflect on my own experience of using the five stages of loss to create a structured way of dealing with my own grief. In that regard, the five stages served me well in the following ways.

When I was unexpectedly confronted with the death of my wife, Veta, I found it astounding that there was no suitable guide to help me get through the deep grief of losing her. While *Grief* described what I might expect to experience, illustrated with examples from the lives of real people, it did not inform me how to plan for or otherwise manage my grief. Indeed, nothing I had read previously or in the aftermath of when Veta died suggested that grief could be somehow managed. Since such grief is a quintessential part of human experience, I would have thought that we would be much more adept at guiding ourselves through it, but we are not. My hope, therefore, is that this work will serve as such a guide.

Though *Grief* was not structured as a guide, the five stages of loss described by Kübler-Ross and Kessler in *Grief* nonetheless proved to be a simple and highly useful place to begin. I could understand what aspect of grief each stage was attempting to describe; I could easily work the stages into my calendar; and the stages were presented in *Grief* with sufficient conditional language and caveats that I was not tempted to treat them as absolute truth.

So for me under the circumstances, the stages of loss provided an adequate conceptual foundation—the five stages—for the emotional challenge I was facing, even if I had to develop my own structure for getting through it.

In addition, in retrospect I found that the stages were a reasonable match for my own journey through loss. The authors of *Grief* clearly indicated that there is "not a typical response to loss" (*Grief*, 7). And indeed, the stages of loss do not in every case describe precisely what I felt. They were, however, close enough to give me a way to set my expectations and to put meaningful names on what I was feeling.

I also found the sequence to be roughly correct. I did not experience an orderly and sharp progression from one stage to the next, and the authors of *Grief* did not lead me to believe that I would. There were fits and starts among my emotions as I grieved. *Disbelief*, in particular, would resurface as I worked on subsequent stages. Its resurfacing, however, would be progressively shorter in duration and impact, and the stage I was working through at the time would continue to occupy my thoughts and feelings. In addition, I didn't fully experience the third stage, *bargaining*. But stopping to reflect on the idea represented by the bargaining stage was immensely useful in helping me recover an important aspect of my past that I had repressed or otherwise forgotten. So, differences notwithstanding, I found the sequencing of the stages to be generally on target in helping prepare me for the feelings that were coming.

Without the stages as a starting place, I believe that my grief would have seemed much more chaotic and puzzling. Just being able to name and anticipate feelings and knowing that such feelings are common among those who are grieving gave me a sense of normalcy even in my darkest moments. The stages also gave me a degree of control that helped me continue to function in my professional role without fear of neglecting my grieving.

For these reasons, it is my conclusion that Kübler-Ross and Kessler's work identifying five stages of loss was, for me, generally accurate, very usable, and exceedingly valuable as a basic tool for developing my grief calendar.

Grief Storms. Though Kübler-Ross and Kessler discuss the matter of episodes of crying, I believe a greater emphasis should be placed on what they discussed under the heading "Tears" (*Grief*, 42–47). Based on my experience and what I have been told by others, I think the phenomenon of being swept up in a wave of emotion is sufficiently universal and frequent that it deserves more attention. I settled on the descriptive phrase *Grief Storm* to describe the common experience of suddenly bursting into tears that happens throughout the five stages of loss and sometimes beyond. Grief storms can be precipitated by almost anything: opening a drawer and finding something that belonged to the departed, hearing a song that was special for him or her, or visiting a place where you had been together. A grief storm can accompany deep sadness, fond memories, or simply being surprised.

During my grieving, I experienced grief storms frequently. I decided early on simply to let them run their course when possible. When it was not possible, especially in public settings where breaking down in tears would be conspicuous or inappropriate, I usually managed to ride out the storm, sometimes tearing up without breaking down. When it was possible to let the tears flow, the episodes were intense but relatively brief. They were occasions where I went through a lot of tissues, sometimes crying almost uncontrollably.

Though at first I did not like them and, even when alone, was somewhat embarrassed by them, I eventually came to view them as important and therapeutic. As a result, I began to use them (after they had subsided) as occasions to ask myself where I was in the grief process and how I was doing. I wanted to understand each time what had triggered the storm and why.

In the long run, therefore, I found grief storms helpful both for releasing emotional tension and for aiding me in assessing where I was in my progress in the grief process.

Managing Grief. Looking back on my sojourn through the

grief process, I am all the more convinced that grief, even the most intense grief, will be a more constructive and eventually positive experience if it is engaged with a general idea of what to expect and at least a loose plan for dealing with it. The outline of a plan I suggest in chapter 1 consists of the following:

- Make the decision to live!
- Get a sense, an understanding, of what you will be feeling.
- Create your personal calendar for dealing with the stages of loss.
- Set aside regular times to think and reflect on your grief and begin today.
- Strongly consider having a memorial service, funeral, or other formal means of celebrating your loved one's life.
- Don't drown out your grief with TV, music, web surfing, or other forms of distraction.
- Don't turn to alcohol or drugs as a solace for emotional pain.
- Don't hesitate to get help.
- Take care of the practical tasks.

What is important in creating your plan to deal with your loss is that it fit your personal situation and personal style and that you set your intention on getting through your grief.

Growth. It was about two months after I had moved through the five stages of loss and finished my grief calendar that I had the conversation that led to writing this account. As I began the process of writing, I had a recurrence of the distinct feeling that the agonizing process of going through deep grief had prepared me for a new level of growth and maturity. Though I had intentionally aimed for such growth as a result of my heart surgeries, when I thought about growth as a result of Veta's death, I was consciously uncomfortable; it clearly seemed wrong to feel that way.

Now in retrospect, it seems to me that almost any life experience that we go through with self-awareness and mindfulness can contribute to our intellectual growth, our emotional maturity, and sometimes both. This is especially true if we take time to revisit the experience carefully and thoughtfully. In this case, even the most difficult experience, one I would have done virtually anything to prevent, has had that effect on me.

While creating a grief calendar and attempting to go through the grief process deliberately began as an act of desperation on my part, it had the unanticipated value of heightening my self-awareness and causing me to engage in reading and reflection regularly throughout. This, combined with the effort to write about the experience, has certainly felt to me like a personal growth process.

As a result, while I have for many years been comfortable with the idea of my own mortality, I believe that I am now much better able to deal with the death of others and to help others through their own grief. I have a much better understanding, for instance, that there is no magic thing to say to make someone in grief suddenly feel better. In the past, even though I knew better, I always searched my mind for just the right thing to say in order to make the person dealing with loss feel better. As I now know from personal experience, trying to do so is a misguided goal. Only time, grieving, and healing will ease the person's discomfort. It is rather the simple fact of being present and supportive that does the most good—a valuable lesson I learned from my friends.

I make this observation about growth in part to argue

that it gives credence to the value of approaching grief in an organized way with an agenda to derive the most positive outcome possible from one of the most devastating experiences common to the human family. For me, the simple awareness of the stages and the soft "deadlines" for them in my calendar functioned in an almost subliminal manner to help me move through them in a self-conscious way, and I believe they can serve the same function for others. With a little forethought and some help from a book like *Grief*, not only can we survive great loss but we can also come to understand ourselves better as a result of it.

I think this positive momentum could have occurred as a result of reflecting on my grief, whether or not I had intended to write about it. I also think it is likely that many people experience such a growth stage as a result of thinking back on their grief, talking with friends about it, journaling, or some other personally suitable way of summing it up or putting it in perspective.

If I were to be creating a grief calendar for myself now, I would add a stage six and call it *Growth*. I characterize growth as a time at the end of five stages when one thinks back through the grief process as a way of consciously bringing it to a constructive conclusion and setting one's sights toward the future. For me, the notion of stage five acceptance was not constructive in that it did not provide a positive momentum. Rather, it felt like a kind of begrudging acknowledgement of the finality of Veta's death. When the lid on the box for my wedding band snapped shut, I knew a big chapter in my life had closed, but I did not feel an enthusiasm for what would come next.

The additional reflection that occurred as a result of preparing to write this account, however, not only provided me with new insights about myself but also gave me the sense of enthusiasm that had been lacking. In terms of new insights about myself, it seems that working through the stages of loss was mostly about dealing with the ordeal of loss and just getting through the various emotions evoked by the process. It was not until I sat down to write about it that I had the emotional distance to understand myself better through the lenses of those emotions. I also began to understand better how my physical struggles have shaped how I deal emotionally, intellectually, and spiritually with life.

In addition, the reflection and writing allowed me to push back a bit from my involvement in the story and understand that the story told here is so much more than just my grieving process, the grief calendar, and that book on which the grief calendar is based. It is a salute to the life of an extraordinary woman and a witness about how a community pulls together to express its own grief and help one of its own grieve after her loss.

It was tempting when I suffered the loss of Veta, to privatize the experience, to become lost in self-pity. What I have called the growth stage allowed me to accept and internalize an awareness that the whole experience was not just about me. It is also about the universal struggle we humans have dealing with death, how our very identity changes when someone we love dies, and how our struggle with our understanding of a reality we call "God" is lifelong.

But perhaps the most important contribution for me from the growth stage was my rediscovery of the zest for life. Going back through my grief, remembering and writing about Veta, reflecting on family and friends, recalling how good and positive our life had been—somehow this restored my hope for what life still might hold for me. I found new enthusiasm for life out of the process of dealing with what for me has been life's greatest loss.

I believe the opportunity for growth resulting from loss is there for anyone who approaches the grief process in a deliberate and thoughtful way and then makes a retrospective effort to review and understand the experience. It is worth the effort; it is when you will know that you made the right decision in choosing to live.

38826959R00089

Made in the USA
Lexington, KY
31 January 2015